115658

REASON
AND REVELATION

Also by Richard H. Akeroyd

The Spiritual Quest of Albert Camus
Madeleine and André Gide (translator with foreword)
The Door
The Flock and the Kingdom
He Made Us a Kingdom
He Is Nigh
Through the Scent of Water
Called and Chosen and Faithful
Elisha, or Ministry to the Second Generation
The Lord's Servant
The Word, the Churches, and the Work
The Cage with the Open Door:
A Pneumabiography of André Gide

REASON
AND REVELATION

From Paul
to Pascal

by

Richard H. Akeroyd

115658

ISBN 0-86554-405-0 (paper)
ISBN 0-86554-386-0 (casebound)

REASON
AND REVELATION
From Paul to Pascal
Copyright ©1991
Mercer University Press
Macon, Georgia 31207 USA
All rights reserved
Printed in the United States of America

The paper used in this publication
meets the minimum requirements of American National
Standard for Information Services—Permanence of Paper
for Printed Library Materials, ANSI Z39.48-1984.

LIBRARY OF CONGRESS CATALOGING-IN-PUBLICATION DATA
Akeroyd, Richard H., 1921–
Reason and revelation : from Paul to Pascal
by Richard H. Akeroyd.
ix + 130 pp.   6 × 9″ (15 × 23cm.)
Includes bibliographical references and index.
ISBN 0-86554-386-0 (alk. paper)
1. Faith and reason—History of doctrines. 2. Revelation—
History of doctrines. 3. Philosophy, French. I. Title.
BT50.A24   1991
231.7′4′09—dc20
91-18226
CIP

Contents

Preface

When he was still in his early twenties, says André Gide, the embryo of each of the works he would subsequently write was already there, dormant in the back of his mind, occasionally evidencing its presence by surfacing into the active consciousness but, for the most part, waiting its turn unobtrusively in the wings. For many years it has been ''on my mind'' to trace in broad outline the history of the influence of revelation, contrasting it with that of reason functioning independently from revelation, starting from the advent of Christianity and extending down to Pascal, also reaching forward briefly to include Jean-Jacques Rousseau. But revelation is so intangible—as I circled it, the handle eluded me. Then it dawned—the properties of sunlight are best understood from its effects; radiation cannot be perceived by the senses, but its consequences can be measured. Even so, the history of the part that revelation, or the lack of it, has played in the lives of men can be best understood from an analysis of their manner of thinking, their approach to thought, their minds.

This book is therefore a sequential study of representative minds. First, of the apostle Paul who, at his dramatic conversion, became instantly aware of another dimension which he was subsequently to understand to be the ''mind of Christ.'' Then the long stretch of theological disputation through the Middle Ages, starting with Augustine who was released and launched into his ministry as a consequence of revelation, and ending with Thomas Aquinas for whom, alas, the revelation followed the ministry. Montaigne appears to have accepted the fact of revelation (to have indicated otherwise would have been tantamount to blasphemy in his day), but seemed little concerned by his lack of experience of it. Descartes separated his religious life from the intellectual, and set himself to demonstrate by means of the latter the validity of the former. Finally, there is Pascal—whom I shall treat in some detail—who paradoxically seems to evince the traits of most of the foregoing types of mind in various of his writings. As a postscript Rousseau appears to have learned from the vagaries of the past and to be on the right scent, but then, in a fit of petulance, he flounders, and what had seemed to be a progression in pure spiritual perception turns out to be flawed by romantic nostalgia.

Any mind is a complex universe, and I am fully aware of the dangers of categorizing too abruptly. Yet, in some instances, the genus is clear and, in the case of Paul, even defined by him. With others the frontiers are less sharply delineated; nevertheless, comparison yields distinctions.

What will issue from this study? That, in the history of Christian thought, there have emerged three general categories of minds—the spiritual, the mystical and the intellectual. That the mystical and the intellectual each offer an abnormal, less than wholesome, and incomplete representation of true Christianity, each emanating from one aspect of man's nature only; whereas the spiritual, integrating all aspects of man's nature into a unity, conveys both a normality and a completeness—all that manhood before God is intended to be.

There are two distinct forms of revelation. All wisdom is, in a sense, revealed and not learned. It comes to those who are of a quiet, sensitive spirit, and gently asserts itself with the passage of time as experience of life confirms. "Experience has taught me" confided an eminent Oxford philosopher over a cup of tea, "that by the intellectual exercise of our reason we can circle the truth, but never reach it."—"There is some value in the exercise, however," he added rather wistfully, "for the development of students' thinking processes." But the Revelation of Jesus Christ is altogether other. There may be, and usually is, a long period of preparation prior to it, but, when it comes, there is a complete reorientation of the life as to authority. "No man" says the apostle Paul "can say, Jesus is Lord, but in the Holy Spirit" (1 Cor 12:3).

———————————

It should be mentioned that the version of the Bible quoted here and throughout the text is, unless otherwise noted, that of the (English) Revised Version (R.V., 1881, 1885, 1895); the initials A.T. indicate the text quoted is according to the author's translation.

Acknowledgements

I wish to express my gratitude to Penguin Books of London, England, for permission to quote from *Confessions* by Saint Augustine, translated and copyrighted (1961) by R. S. Pine-Coffin; and from *The Imitation of Christ* by Thomas à Kempis, translated and copyrighted (1952) by Leo Sherley-Price. The Encyclopaedia Britannica kindly granted permission for me to quote from the article on "Mysticism" in *Encyclopaedia Britannica,* 14th edition (1957). Random House, Inc., allowed that I quote from *Montaigne* by André Gide. William Morrow and Company, insofar as their authority allows, granted me permission to quote from *Pascal* by Morris Bishop (1936, Reynal and Hitchcock). Garnier Frères gave permission for me to quote from the "Classiques Garnier" edition of *Lettres Philosophiques* by Voltaire, *Pensées* by Pascal, and *Confessions* by J.-J. Rousseau. Although the work is in the public domain, MacMillan Publishing Company asked that I give credit to Charles Scribner's Sons for my quotations from *A Select Library of the Nicene and Post Nicene Fathers of the Christian Church,* volume 8 (1908). Whilst stating that no formal permission was necessary for my quotation from *Aquinas* by Anthony Kenny, Farrar, Straus and Giroux Inc., did ask that I acknowledge the book, published by Hill and Wang in New York in 1980. The Crossroad/Continuum Publishing Group kindly granted me permission to quote from *The Agony of Christianity* by Unamuno (Ungar, 1960), and from *The Creed of a Priest of Savoy* by Jean-Jacques Rousseau (translated by Arthur H. Beattie; Ungar, 1956). Alfred A. Knopf Inc. kindly granted me permission to publish my translation of the brief excerpts from Camus and Saint-Exupéry, which appear in the first chapter.

CHAPTER 1

Paul
and the
"Mind of Christ"

————//————

Tarsus was a notable city when Paul was born there some time during the early years of the first century A.D. Following a distinguished history of approximately 1,000 years, the city had grown to a population of about a half million. In 334 B.C., on his campaign to the East which was to end with his death in Babylon some eleven years later, Alexander the Great passed through the city and thereafter the predominant influence was Greek. In 41 B.C. Cleopatra sailed into Tarsus and thence up the Cydnus river on her way to woo and win Mark Antony. In Paul's day the city boasted a respected University which numbered among its scholars the famous Stoic philosopher Athenodorus.

Jews had settled in Tarsus, particularly during the early part of the second century B.C. when they were offered citizenship if they took up residence. Paul's ancestors probably emigrated to Tarsus at this time, and he inherited this local citizenship from them (Acts 21:39). When later the Romans occupied the city, following the division of Alexander's empire upon his death, the occasion arose for one of Paul's forbears either to purchase Roman citizenship or to receive it as a reward for some service performed in the interest of Rome or of one of her citizens. This citizenship Paul inherited also (Acts 22:25-28).

In his home, the child Saul (following his conversion, he was referred to by his Latin/Roman name Paulus; previously, by his Hebrew name Saul) probably spoke Aramaic in which he was fluent (Acts 22:2—the "Hebrew dialect" being Aramaic). His letters are evidence of his proficiency in Greek, and his quotations from the Old Testament, often from memory, suggest his knowledge of Hebrew or at least of the Greek translation of the Hebrew Scriptures (the Septuagint). Apparently he received his early formal education either at home or in a school connected to the synagogue. In his youth (probably early teens) he was sent to Jerusalem (Acts 26:4) where he studied under the great Gamaliel (Acts 22:3), the grandson of Hillel, each of whom had been the most revered expositor of the Law and the Hebrew Scriptures of his day. The Mishna comments that "since Rabban Gamaliel the elder died there has been no more reverence for the Law."[1]

Saul studied the Law and was devoted to it, priding himself on being a Pharisee in its defense (Phil 3:5). One may assume he did not participate in the persecution of Jesus of Nazareth (he perhaps never even saw him); otherwise, when expressing remorse at having persecuted the saints (1 Cor 15:9), he probably would have mentioned having persecuted their Lord also.

Some believe Paul's early devotion and brilliance were rewarded by a seat in the Sanhedrin, the Jews' supreme governing body in those days; others dispute this. It is recorded, however, that when Stephen was martyred, Paul not only was present but played a responsible role in directing the proceedings (Acts 7:58).

Some of the most influential of the Jews at this time advised a course of tolerance towards Christianity, hoping that if the movement was treated as a Jewish sect it would soon pass its peak and be absorbed. Gamaliel, tutor and mentor of Saul, was a leading proponent of this policy (Acts 5:34-39); but his student would have none of it. "Saul, yet breathing threatening and slaughter against the disciples of the Lord, went unto the high priest, and asked of him letters to Damascus unto the synagogues, that if he found any that were of the Way, whether men or women, he might bring them

---

[1] As quoted in F. F. Bruce, *The Acts of the Apostles: The Greek Text with Introduction and Commentary* (Grand Rapids MI: Eerdmans, 1951) 146.

bound to Jerusalem." (Acts 9:1-2) There is usually some explanation for behavior which is so extreme, and Saul's case here is no exception. It is unquestionable that, as he directed the stoning of Stephen, he was profoundly affected by what he heard and saw. At the beginning of Stephen's defense before the Sanhedrin, it is recorded that his face was "as it had been the face of an angel" (Acts 6:15). When he finished his defense, those assembled "were cut to the heart and they gnashed on him with their teeth. But he, being full of the Holy Ghost, looked up steadfastly into heaven, and saw the glory of God, and Jesus standing on the right hand of God, and said, Behold, I see the heavens opened, and the Son of Man standing on the right hand of God" (Acts 7:54-56). Unable to contain themselves any longer, the infuriated persecutors "cried out with a loud voice, and stopped their ears, and rushed upon him with one accord; and they cast him out of the city, and stoned him" (Acts 7:57-58). As Stephen died, it was as if, in the Spirit, Christ lived again and acted through him, expressing the same sentiments as on the cross: "Lord Jesus, receive my spirit. . . . Lord, lay not this sin to their charge" (Acts 7:59-60). It is impossible to witness such a sight and hear such words and remain untouched. For one such as Saul there were but two alternatives, either to capitulate or to multiply fury and frenzied activity in an attempt to blind oneself to what one has seen and drown out what one has heard. Saul hurled himself into this latter course.

Happily, some of the most vociferous, exhibiting the greatest animosity, are the most vulnerable; such was the case with Saul. His journey to Damascus was in fact a last-gasp, desperate effort to escape back to the religious status quo he had formerly known by eliminating Christianity and thus, hopefully, freeing himself from his conscience which, since the death of Stephen, had given him no rest. But, unknown to him, he was now prepared—a candidate for higher things. "Suddenly there shone round about him a light out of heaven." (Acts 9:3) And when he entered Damascus, probably later the same day, it was not as the chief persecutor of Christians but as the humblest Christian brother (Acts 9:17). A diametric turn around of 180 degrees. All of Paul's preconceptions and prejudgments were swept away in an instant by a spiritual encounter with one he thought to be dead. From this moment onwards, the rest of Paul's life, which was continuous ministry, was to be governed by this encounter and its issue. Whereas his *mind* had been such that he "verily thought with [himself] that [he] ought to do many things contrary to the name of Jesus of Nazareth" (Acts 26:9), such a radical transformation had taken place that he can now say, "We have the *mind of Christ*" (1 Cor 2:16).

What did Paul mean by the *mind* (νοῦς *nous*) of Christ?

The best way to answer this question is to look first at all the Greek words—there are six—that translators of the New Testament have sometimes translated as "mind," and then to examine more precisely those occasions where Paul specifically uses this word *nous*, as in the quotation above.

1. ψυχή *psuche*

"lest ye be wearied and faint in your mind" (Heb 12:3 Authorized Version, hereafter A.V.). This is rightly corrected in the English Revised Version (hereafter R.V.) to read "in your souls."

2. γνώμη *gnōmē*

"but without thy mind would I do nothing" (Phm 14 A.V.). Also rendered "mind" in the R.V., meaning "opinion" or "judgment."

3. νόημα *noēma*

"the god of this world hath blinded the minds of them which believe not" (2 Cor 4:4 A.V.). "Mind" is also used in the R.V., but a marginal note indicates rightly that the Greek means "thoughts."

4. φρόνημα *phronēma*

"To be carnally minded is death; but to be spiritually minded is life and peace" (Rom 8:6 A.V.). Rendered more literally in the R.V.: "the mind of the flesh is death, but the mind of the spirit is life and peace." Here the word means "inclination" or "disposition."

5. διάνοια *dianoia*

"I will put my laws into their mind . . . and in their minds will I write them" (Heb 8:10, 10:16 A.V.). "Mind" also appears in the R.V., *dianoia* here indicating the "intellect" or "thinking processes."

6. νοῦς *nous*

"we have the mind of Christ" (1 Cor 2:16, A.V. and R.V.). *Nous* appears twenty-one times in Paul's writings. In both the A.V. and R.V. it is translated sixteen times as "mind" and five times as "understanding."

What is the nature and content of this mind (*nous*) of Christ? What role does it play? How does it come to be in the believer? It is significant that

Paul does not use any of the other five words listed above to express this concept. It is not an "opinion" (*gnōmē*—2) or mere "thoughts" (*noēma*—3) that he is speaking of. Nor is it just an attitude or a "disposition" (*phronēma*—4). It certainly is not "intellect" (*dianoia* —5).

We can now examine certain key statements in which the apostle uses *nous* and, from them, build up a composite understanding of the meaning he intended by this word.

1. "This I say therefore, and testify in the Lord, that ye no longer walk as the Gentiles also walk, in the vanity of their mind (*nous*), being darkened in their understanding (*dianoia*), alienated from the life of God because of the ignorance that is in them, because of the hardness of their heart." (Eph 4:17)

   The heart governs. If it is hardened, then there will be alienation from God's life which will result in the "thinking processes," the "intellect," (*dianoia*) being frustrated, as it seeks to operate in a context which lacks a necessary dimension—light. Also the mind (*nous*), the purpose, bent, focus, being thereby dissociated from anything that has ultimate meaning, will only lead in vanity—emptiness.

2. "And even as they refused to have God in their knowledge, God gave them up unto a reprobate mind (*nous*) to do those things which are not fitting." (Rom 1:28)

   "Be not fashioned according to this world (age): but be ye transformed by the renewing of your mind (*nous*), that ye may prove what is the good and acceptable and perfect will of God." (Rom 12:2)

   On the one hand, spiritual disobedience, the refusal to give God His place in the inner counsels of the heart, provokes Him to abandon to their own deserts those who act thus. Their minds (*nous*), no longer anchored, become reprobate (*adokimos*—inadequate to pass the test), and their condition is evidenced by acts which are not fitting.

   On the other hand, in the case of those who present their bodies as a living sacrifice to God (Rom 12:1), the mind (*nous*) will pass through a metamorphosis, having something new (not recent but different—*anakainoō*) added to it. Such will not be fashioned according to this age but will enter into the experience of the will of God.

3. " . . . vainly puffed up by his fleshly mind (*nous*)." (Col 2:18)

   " . . . be renewed (to make young, recent not different—*ananeoō*) in the spirit of your mind (*nous*)." (Eph 4:23)

The mind can thus yield to the influence of either the flesh or the spirit. The former induces puffing up whereas the latter rejuvenates.

Here I must digress as we find a close correspondence between the place the "mind" occupies in relation to the spirit on the one hand and to the body on the other, and the place of the "soul."

Paul conceived of man's nature as being tripartite—body, soul and spirit (1 Thess 5:23). The person is essentially the soul (Israel was numbered by "souls" [Ex 1:5], and this practice continued in England until at least the twelfth Century); the body is the medium through which the person associates with this earth; and the person communicates with God through his spirit—"the spirit of the man which is in him" (1 Cor 2:11)—linking the soul with the Spirit of God.

The unregenerate man has a spirit, and will sometimes, without consciously identifying it, sense the presence of the Spirit of God. The regenerate man has come back home, as it were, and if he is wise, submits in continual obedience to what he had formerly only occasionally sensed.

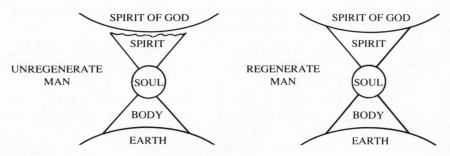

(Possessing the additional faculty of a spirit distinguishes man from the animals: "Among men, who knows what a man is but the man's own spirit within him." [1 Cor 2:11 NEB] Thus man, when he fears that other men may perceive his guilty conscience, seeks solace in communion with his dog which cannot discern.)

According to the figure above, the "mind" (*nous*) occupies much the same position as the "soul." Yet they are distinct because

4. "I delight in the law of God after the inward man: but I see a different law in my members, warring against the law of my mind (*nous*), and bringing me into captivity under the law of sin which is in my members. O wretched man that I am! Who shall deliver me out of this body of death? I thank God through Jesus Christ Our Lord. So then I myself with

the mind (*nous*) serve the law of God; but with the flesh the law of sin."
(Rom 7:22)

Sinful appetites, in which the soul has indulged and which it has permitted to become ensconced in the flesh, now resist the mind (*nous*), which
knows better, and they prove to be too strong for it. The remedy is through
Jesus Christ Our Lord.

Sanctification is the process by which the soul and the flesh become
tamed, subject to the "mind of Christ" which is in the believer, and in
harmony with it. The more deeply this process is permitted to develop, the
more closely the "mind" of the one being sanctified approximates to the
"mind of Christ." The believer receives this "mind" in embryo at regeneration; it then unfolds, develops and occupies as the process of sanctification is permitted to proceed.

Further evidence of the distinction between the "mind" (*nous*) and the
"soul" (*psucheē*) can be seen in the following passage relating to speaking
in tongues.

5. "If I pray in a tongue, my spirit prayeth, but my understanding (*nous*)
   is unfruitful. What is it then? I will pray with the spirit, and I will pray
   with the understanding (*nous*) also: I will sing with the spirit, and I will
   sing with the understanding (*nous*) also. . . . in the church I had rather
   speak five words with my understanding (*nous*), that I might profit others also, than ten thousand words in a tongue." (1 Cor 14:14, 15, 19)

Speaking in a tongue thus bypasses the mind (*nous*). What is uttered
is unintelligible both to the speaker and to the hearer—the mind (*nous*) is
excluded from any part in it. It is unimaginable that the soul also could
likewise be totally set aside. In fact, there is always an element, to a greater
or lesser degree, of emotion or soul force, in each instance of the phenom-
enon of speaking in tongues, or in anything else that man says or does. It
is significant that Paul uses (*nous*) here and not just (*dianoia*)—the "intellect," or *noēma*—the "thoughts."

Finally, taking a little further what was mentioned in paragraph 4 regarding there being a stage of development, a measure of the maturity of
the mind,

6. "One man esteemeth one day above another: another esteemeth every
   day alike. Let each man be fully assured in his own mind (*nous*)." (Rom
   14:5) ". . . be not quickly shaken from your mind (*nous*)." (2 Thess
   2:2)

I am all too conscious of the wisdom of Baudelaire's warning that he had tried more than once, as had all his friends, to shut himself up in a system so as to be able to preach from within it at his ease. But a system is a sort of damnation, he said. He returned to seeking shelter in impeccable naïveté. It is there that his philosophical conscience found rest. Yet there is enough for us here—while eschewing the temptation to conclude too soon and categorize too distinctly—nevertheless to formulate a good idea of what Paul meant by *nous*. We can say broadly that, to him,

> all experiences, encounters, things read and heard, create an impression and conspire to produce a level of knowledge. This in turn is shaped and colored by the desires, lusts, appetites and ambitions, on the one hand; or ordered and set in proper focus by revelation of spiritual reality on the other. The resultant wisdom and spiritual perception, or lack of it, focussing into an attitude and outlook, could be called the *nous*.

But how does all this apply to Paul himself?

It is not in boast when he writes to the Galatians, "Ye have heard of my manner of life in time past. . . . I advanced in the Jew's religion beyond many of mine own age among my countrymen, being more exceedingly zealous for the traditions of my fathers" (Gal 1:13); or to the Philippians, "circumcised the eighth day, of the stock of Israel, of the tribe of Benjamin, a Hebrew of Hebrews; as touching the law of a Pharisee . . . ; as touching the righteousness which is in the law, found blameless" (Phil 3:5). Before Agrippa, Paul testified, "My manner of life from my youth up, which was from the beginning among mine own nation, and at Jerusalem, know all the Jews; having knowledge of me from the first, if they be willing to testify, how that after the strictest sect of our religion I lived a Pharisee" (Acts 26:4). Nevertheless, despite this exemplary upbringing and, on his part, devotion, his mind (*nous*) was such that, "I verily thought with myself, that I ought to do many things contrary to the name of Jesus of Nazareth. And this I also did in Jerusalem: and I both shut up many of the saints in prisons, having received authority from the chief priests, and when they were put to death, I gave my vote against them. And punishing them oftentimes in all the synagogues, I strove to make them blaspheme; and being exceedingly mad against them, I persecuted them even unto foreign cities" (Acts 26:9). But he had an explanation, if not an excuse, for having acted thus: "I did it ignorantly in unbelief" (1 Tim 1:13).

PAUL AND THE "MIND OF CHRIST"

PAUL AND THE "MIND OF CHRIST"

What essentially happened to Paul on the Damascus road was that his mind (*nous*) became suddenly awakened to another dimension. He had learned to live in his reason and intellect, logically applying the tenets of Judaism to life as he saw it; and now, of a sudden, he hears a voice: "Why persecutest thou me?" He asks, "Who art thou Lord?" and receives the reply, "I am Jesus whom thou persecutest" (Acts 26:15). He had thought that he was just persecuting the members of a heretical sect, but now the spiritual reality of the Body of Christ dawns upon him—when he reached out and laid his hands on Christians he touched Jesus Christ. Whereas he had "verily thought [he] ought to do many things contrary to the name of Jesus of Nazareth," he now awakens to how those actions appeared to God: the lid is taken off his mind (*nous*), as it were. He had formerly seen everything horizontally and was only conscious of the world his physical eyes could see around him; now, in an instant, he is not only conscious of the reality and presence of God, but sees things from His standpoint. He later describes this inner revolution: "When it was the good pleasure of God . . . to reveal His Son in me" (Gal 1:15). From the moment of this crisis, this new spiritual orientation of Paul's mind (*nous*) becomes the rule for all his spiritual service: whenever he speaks or writes about anything, which touches upon God or the nature of man, this orientation governs, and he never descends to horizontal intellectual disputation.

There is a momentary slip during Paul's final visit to Jerusalem when he engages first in a battle of wits with Pharisees and Sadducees in the Council (Acts 23:6) and later with Festus (Acts 25:10). I have dealt in some detail with the circumstances that led up to this crisis, and the consequences of it, in the last chapter of my book *Through the Scent of Water*, and there is no need to reiterate here. That Paul became fully reestablished in his spiritual mind (*nous*) is quite clear from the spiritual measure of the epistles he later wrote from prison in Rome (Ephesians, Philippians, and Colossians).

Albert Camus perceives the difference between the spiritual mind and the intellectual, writing in the introduction to his M.A. thesis,

> In the paintings in the catacombs, the good shepherd gladly adopts the face of Hermes. But if the smile is the same, the meaning of the symbol has changed. Thus it is that Christian thought, constrained to express itself in a coherent system, tried to adopt the forms of Greek thought and to express itself in the metaphysical formulae which it found ready-made. . . . One cannot arrive at any idea of what separates Christian dogma and

Greek philosophy by comparing them. It is rather by observing that the realm of the feelings which was native to the evangelical communities is foreign to the classical aspect of Greek sensibility. It is on the emotional level that the problems present themselves, and it is not in the system which tries to answer these problems that one should seek what was different about Christianity. When it first appears, Christianity is not a philosophy, but a harmonious set of aspirations, a faith, which operates within a certain context and seeks its answers within that context.[2]

The realm in which the Greek philosopher's mind functioned is quite other than that of the spiritually enlightened believer of the early Church. It was a mistake when, in his zeal to make Christianity understandable to those on the outside, the Christian adopted terms and a frame of thought which could not possibly convey the intended meaning to those unaware of the realm of consciousness into which he had been born. Paul resolutely refused to do this and quite candidly acknowledged that the spiritual presentation of Christian truths was, and would always be, foolishness to the unbelieving philosophic mind. He points out that these two realms are mutually exclusive and that confusion is avoided by leaving them so: "seeing that in the wisdom of God the world through its wisdom knew not God, it was God's good pleasure through the foolishness of the preaching to save them that believe. Seeing that the Jews ask for signs, and Greeks seek after wisdom: but we preach Christ crucified, unto Jews a stumbling block and unto Gentiles foolishness" (1 Cor 1:21-23). Thus, when he went to Corinth it was "not with excellency of speech or of wisdom, proclaiming to you the mystery of God. For I determined not to know anything among you, save Jesus Christ, and Him crucified. . . . My speech and my preaching were not in persuasive words of wisdom, but in demonstration of the Spirit and of power: that your faith should not stand in the wisdom of men, but in the power of God" (1 Cor 2:1-5). Much (how much?) of theology is none other than the intrusion of the philosophic mind into the things of God.

To Paul there are three possible levels of consciousness. (1) That of the *natural* man (ψυχικός *psuchikos,* of the soul, "soulical," 1 Cor 2:14). This is the lowest; any communication with animals will be at this level, and also any communication between men which disregards the spiritual

[2]Albert Camus, *Essais,* intro. par R. Quilliot, édition établie et annotée par R. Quilliot et L. Fauçon, Bibliothèque de la Pléiade 183 (Paris: Éditions Gallimard, 1965) 1224 (A.T.).

nature of man and the mutual respect that this calls for. (2) That of the man who is in tune with the *spirit of the man* that is in him (1 Cor 2:11), and who consequently knows "the things of a man." Saint-Exupéry saw clearly the distinction between these first two:

> I am struck by a fact that no one acknowledges: the life of the Spirit is intermittent, it comes and goes. The life of the intelligence, it alone is permanent, or more or less so. There are very few variations in my faculties of analysis. The Spirit does not occupy itself with things but rather with the sense or meaning which ties them together—it is another face which lies back of them. The Spirit passes directly from full and open vision to absolute blindness.[3]

(3) That of the spiritual man who has received the Spirit of God that he "might know the things that are freely given to us by God" (1 Cor 2:12).

I conclude this chapter by quoting the whole passage from which the above excerpts are taken. The passage is as it appears in *The New English Bible* except that I have substituted "soulical" (ψυχικός *psuchikos*) for "a man who is unspiritual." Spirit with a capital-S indicates the Spirit of God, whereas the lowercase-s indicates the spirit of the man which is in him.

> For the Spirit explores everything, even the depths of God's own nature. Among men, who knows what a man is but the man's own spirit within him? In the same way, only the Spirit of God knows what God is. This is the Spirit that we have received from God, and not the spirit of the world, so that we may know all that God of His own grace gives us; and, because we are interpreting spiritual truths to those who have the Spirit, we speak of these gifts of God in words found for us not by our human wisdom but by the Spirit. A soulical man refuses what belongs to the Spirit of God; it is folly to him; he cannot grasp it, because it needs to be judged in the light of the Spirit. A man gifted with the Spirit can judge the worth of everything, but is not himself subject to judgment by his fellowmen. For (in the words of Scripture) "who knows the mind of the Lord? Who can advise Him?" We, however, possess the mind of Christ. (1 Cor 2:10-16)

---

[3]Antoine-Marie-Roger de Saint-Exupéry, *Oeuvres*, pref. de Roger Caillois, Bibliothèque de la Pléiade 98 (Paris: Éditions Gallimard, 1959) 275 (A.T.).

CHAPTER 2

Augustine
to Aquinas

———————— // ————————

"And the Word made Himself flesh and dwelled among us, and we saw His glory, glory such as belongs to the only-begotten Son of the Father." Thus we read in the Prologue of the Gospel according to John (1:14). And this Word, Who made Himself flesh, died after His passion, after His agony, and then the Word turned into the letter.[1]

The apostasy, the falling away from the reality of true Christianity, begins for Unamuno with the death of Christ. Paul sealed the first stage of the decline, turning "the evangelical into the biblical, the Word into the letter."[2] Augustine represents the next step, he was "the man of the letter . . . already a jurist, a legalist. So was St. Paul, who was simultaneously a mystic—a man in whom the mystic and the jurist were at war. On one side stood the law, on the other side grace."[3]

Unamuno's is an extreme position: he believes "Christianity is incom-

---

[1] Miguel de Unamuno, *The Agony of Christianity*, trans. Kurt F. Reinhardt (New York: Frederick Ungar, 1960) 36.

[2] Ibid., 42.

[3] Ibid., 80.

municable.''[4] While many would agree with him that "reason is entirely powerless to penetrate to the heart of the mysteries of faith,"[5] there must surely be but few who would hold with him and Keyserling that "the living Christ would have found neither Paul nor Augustine nor Calvin among His followers."[6] Unamuno appears to discount entirely any possibility of the Spirit working through the written word: "The spirit, the breath, which is word and oral tradition imparts life, but the letter, which is bookish, kills."[7] And this off-center focus of the intellectual mystic, who summarily dismisses the intellect in spiritual things, leads him into his agony. Like Kierkegaard, he becomes obsessed with the contrary conclusions reached by reason and faith. He magnifies what he believes to be an anomaly, examines and probes it from every angle, all the while missing the key, revelation, which so simply resolves the matter.

Here I must repeat a figure I used in my book on Camus.* The blind man can only grope, using his fingers to feel his way in the dark. Should he receive his sight, his reaction would not be to dispense with his fingers but rather that he could now guide them and use them always to profit, the sight delivering them from their fumbling of the past. Even so, spiritual revelation liberates; it puts reason into its right place and looses it to function always helpfully in harmony with the perceptions received.

Camus, who always contended he was not a Christian, is much more cautious than Unamuno. (I am repeatedly amazed by the balance and poise in the expression of Camus's thought—hence its capacity to survive the test of time.) He does not sweep away the intellect, in fact he refuses to negate it when bidden to do so by those who would convert him.[8] But he does affirm—as quoted in chapter 1, above—that "one cannot arrive at any idea of what separates Christian dogma and Greek philosophy by comparing them. . . . When it first appears, Christianity is not a philosophy,

---

[4]Ibid., 6.

[5]Ibid., xxviii.

[6]Ibid., 40.

[7]Ibid., 36.

*Richard H. Akeroyd, *The Spiritual Quest of Albert Camus* (Tuscaloosa AL: Portals Press, 1976) 101.

[8]Albert Camus, *Myth of Sisyphus* (New York: Random House, 1955) 30.

but a harmonious set of aspirations, a faith, which operates within a certain context and seeks its answers within that context.'' Camus recognizes the distinction between the climate of the early Church, which was life and spiritual, and the realm of philosophy which is rational and thus, without revelation, antipathetic to that which is spiritual. In this, his position is essentially similar to that of Paul who wrote, ''The letter killeth, but the Spirit giveth life'' (2 Cor 3:6).

By *letter* Unamuno meant anything written, whereas Paul used the term to indicate a religious law or formula systematically imposed upon man. Paul had been a minister, an officer of the *letter* in the days when he persecuted Christians in his quest to sweep Christianity off the face of the earth. At his conversion he awakened to consciousness of another realm, that of the spirit, of which he had been in ignorance until that moment. Thereafter, in spiritual things, his intellect served as the handmaid of the revelations and perceptions which came to him, giving expression to them and explaining their application to life. These expressions and explanations are not always on the surface and simple (though they are never intellectually complicated); and even the writer of 2 Peter found in Paul ''some things hard to be understood'' (2 Pet 3:16). Nevertheless he recognized the imprimatur of the Spirit of God upon the writings of Paul, attributing Paul's spiritual authority to ''wisdom given to him'' (2 Pet 3:15)—wisdom being of another and higher order than knowledge, conveying the capacity to utilize knowledge helpfully.

Many of Augustine's writings breathe the same spirit as those of Paul. In reading Augustine, one is conscious that the author is giving expression to spiritual perceptions with regard to the Scriptures which have become part of the substratum of his life as a consequence of his spiritual conversion: this is true almost entirely of the *Confessions* and, in large measure, of the *City of God*. In other writings, such as those in opposition to the teachings of Pelagius, there is brilliance of intellect and cleverness of mind, but not the same authority.* It is as if with the former he is on home territory, but with the latter he is ''playing away'' on the opponent's ground; with the former, another and higher authority is with him, but with the latter he is on his own; the former flows vertically with the mind of Christ, but the latter—reason functioning horizontally in independence—must drive. It is this duality, this spiritual schizophrenia, that distinguishes Au-

---

*See appendix A, below, for excerpts from these writings.

gustine from Paul. Can it be explained?

> But while the Word, the *Verbum,* did not write, St. Paul, the Hellenized Jew, the Platonically inspired Pharisee, did write or, more correctly, did dictate his Epistles. In St. Paul the Word turned into letters, the Gospel became a book—the Bible. And thus Protestantism began, and the tyranny of the letter begot St. Augustine. . . .[9]

Though Unamuno's antipathy to anything written is still strong here, there is nevertheless some truth in what he ways. For, step by step, Augustine was disabused with Manichaeism, which he had espoused in his youth, and convinced intellectually of the truth of Christianity, all before the crisis of his spiritual conversion late in his thirty-first year.

AUGUSTINE

Souk-Ahras lies about fifty miles south of the Mediterranean coastal town of Annaba (formerly Bône, Hippo in Augustine's day), in the extreme northeastern corner of present-day Algeria, fifteen miles or so from the Tunisian border. Here Augustine was born in November, 354 A.D.— the city was called Thagaste in those days.

The faith of Augustine's mother Monica has become legendary; but the family was divided spiritually until 370 when his father Patricius, a small landowner and local government official, was converted one year before he died.

In 365, Patricius sent his son away to school in Madaura (now Mdaurouch), about twenty miles from Thagaste, to "study literature and the art of public speaking."[10] Four years later, Augustine returned home to his parents and spent an idle year while his father saved up enough money to send him to school in Carthage, a coastal town in the northeast corner of Tunisia. There was clearly great fondness and mutual respect between father and son, although the latter realized afterwards that, at that time, his father had been unconscious of the spiritual significance of life, and "cared only that I should have a fertile tongue."[11]

---

[9]Unamuno, *The Agony of Christianity,* 40.

[10]Saint Augustine, *Confessions,* trans. R. S. Pine-Coffin (Baltimore: Penguin Classics, 1961) 45.

[11]Ibid., 45.

At Carthage, where his purpose was to study law ("Such ambition was held to be honorable and I determined to succeed in it."[12]), Augustine plunged into a life of sensual satisfaction—he fell in love, attended the theatre, and "sank to the bottom-most depths of skepticism and mockery of devil-worship."[13] But he could never escape an inward spiritual unrest. He read *Hortensius* by Cicero which rekindled his appetite God-ward. So he took up the Scriptures again, but they seemed to him "quite unworthy of comparison with the stately prose of Cicero."[14]

Soon after his arrival at Carthage, after toying briefly with astrology, Augustine developed a growing interest in Manichaeism which was to continue until his twenty-ninth year. This religious movement had been founded a century earlier by Manes, a fanatic who set himself forth as the Paraclete, and was ultimately crucified in Persia in 277 A.D. Manes maintained that Christianity was only partially true: he denied in particular the virgin birth and resurrection of Christ, contending that, since all flesh was tainted with evil, no association whatsoever with it was possible on the part of God. To the spiritually unenlightened mind Manichaeism appeared, in some ways, to offer a logical solution where the Scriptures seemed indefinite. The idea of good and evil, light and darkness, being in conflict, and of all matter being an admixture of the two, seemed eminently thinkable. Affected by his mother's faith and devotion, but unconvinced by her scriptural doctrines, the possessor of a brilliant intellect, highly trained in rhetoric and law, Augustine found Manichaeism appealing, was seduced by its arguments and entered the sect. He never rose above the level of aspirant, however.

Though Manichaeism fascinated him, it did not satisfy, and Augustine continually longed for someone to resolve his problems regarding its teachings. The Manichaeans spoke glowingly to him of their bishop Faustus, whom he waited expectantly to meet.

> For almost the whole of those nine years during which my mind was unsettled and I was an aspirant of the Manichees, I awaited the coming of this man, Faustus, with the keenest expectation. Other members of the sect whom I had happened to meet were unable to answer the questions

---

[12]Ibid., 58.

[13]Ibid., 57.

[14]Ibid., 60.

I raised upon these subjects, but they assured me that once Faustus had
arrived I had only to discuss them with him and he would have no difficulty in giving me a clear explanation of my queries and any other more
difficult problems which I might put forward.[15]

But when Faustus arrived at Carthage it soon became clear to Augustine
that he

> was quite uninformed about the subjects in which I had expected him to
> be an expert, I began to lose hope that he could lift the veil and resolve
> the problems which perplexed me. . . . When I suggested that we should
> consider these problems and discuss them together, he was certainly
> modest enough not to undertake the task. He knew that he did not know
> the answers to my questions and was not ashamed to admit it, for unlike
> many other people whom I have had to endure, he would not try to teach
> me a lesson when he had nothing to say. . . . The keen interest which I
> had had in the Manichean doctrines was checked by this experience, and
> my confidence in the other teachers of the sect was further diminished
> when I saw that Faustus, of whom they spoke so much, was obviously
> unable to settle the numerous problems which troubled me. . . . Once I
> had come to know him [Faustus] well all my endeavors to make progress
> in the sect, as I had intended, were abandoned. I did not cut myself off
> entirely from the Manichees, but as I could find nothing better than the
> beliefs which I had stumbled upon more or less by chance, I decided to
> be content with them for the time being, unless something preferable
> clearly presented itself to me.[16]

Thus Faustus, who had spiritually seduced so many, unwittingly initiated
what was to develop into the release of Augustine from the snare in which
he had been caught.

At the age of twenty-nine, hearing that students in Rome were more
disciplined, Augustine moved there in order to teach in a more academi-
cally conducive atmosphere. In Rome he continued his association with
the Manichaeans, but with less enthusiasm. A year later he moved to Milan
where he was appointed teacher of literature and elocution; and it was there
that he met the Christian bishop Ambrose, who welcomed him as a father
receiving a son.

---

[15]Ibid., 96.

[16]Ibid., 98, 99.

But Augustine was not yet ready to embrace the Christian faith. He went to hear Ambrose speak "to judge for myself whether the reports of his powers as a speaker were accurate, or whether eloquence flowed from him more, or less, readily than I had been told."[17] He was charmed by the older man's delivery and, unwittingly, was led closer to acceptance of the Christian doctrine of salvation.

His [Ambrose's] meaning, which I tried to ignore, found its way into my mind together with his words, which I admired so much. I could not keep the two apart, and while I was all ears to seize upon his eloquence, I also began to sense the truth of what he said, though only gradually. First of all it struck me that it was, after all, possible to vindicate his arguments. I began to believe that the Catholic faith, which I had thought impossible to defend against the objections of the Manichees, might fairly be maintained.[18]

Augustine sensed the inadequacy of reason to resolve the matter, yet it was the only course he knew:

I did not feel that I ought to follow the catholic path simply because it too had its learned men, ready to vouch for it and never at a loss for sound arguments in answer to objections. On the other hand I did not think that my own beliefs should be condemned simply because an equally good case could be made out for either side. For I thought the Catholic side unbeaten but still not victorious. . . . Next I tried my utmost to find some certain proof which would convict the Manichees of falsehood.[19]

But if reason is impotent to convince of the Truth, it is equally powerless, lacking authority, to denounce the error.

At this time Augustine's mother travelled from North Africa to Milan to be with her son who was much impressed by the spontaneous, immediate flow of spiritual life between her and Ambrose. He confessed to her that though not yet a Catholic Christian, at least he was no longer a Manichee. She in turn told him she was sure she would not die before seeing him a faithful Catholic.

Gradually there bore in upon Augustine's consciousness an awareness

---

[17]Ibid., 107.

[18]Ibid., 108.

[19]Ibid., 108.

of the *other* realm, the spiritual, of which Ambrose spoke.

> In his sermons to the people, Ambrose often repeated the text *The written law inflicts death, whereas the spiritual law brings life,* as though this were a rule upon which he wished to insist most carefully. And when he lifted the veil of mystery and disclosed the spiritual meaning of texts which, taken literally, appeared to contain the most unlikely doctrines, I was not aggrieved by what he said, although I did not yet know whether it was true.[20]

But this awareness, interestingly enough, brought apprehension rather than release—he had been solely dependent upon reason for so long that the thought of stepping onto other ground struck fear in him: "I refused to allow myself to accept any of it in my heart, [he is speaking of Ambrose's spiritual exposition of scriptural texts] because I was afraid of a headlong fall, but I was hanging in suspense which was more likely to be fatal than a fall."[21]

But Augustine's confidence in reason was weakened: such an inner reorientation had taken place within him that he now thought it reasonable that

> since we are too weak to discover the truth by reason alone and for this reason need the authority of sacred books, I began to believe that you [God] would never have invested the Bible with such conspicuous authority in every land unless you had intended it to be the means by which we should look for you and believe in you. As for the passages which had previously struck me as absurd, now that I had heard reasonable explanations of many of them I regarded them as of the nature of profound mysteries; and it seemed to me all the more right that the authority of Scripture should be respected and accepted with purest faith, because while all can read it with ease, it also has a deeper meaning in which its great secrets are locked away.[22]

What a paradox! Reason which once renounced Christianity now espousing it.

This turning point was of major import. While Augustine's attitude had

---

[20]Ibid., 116.

[21]Ibid.

[22]Ibid., 117.

been that of a skeptic, his reason found only evidence to refute Christianity; but once the inner reorientation came, apparently imperceptibly to him, faith seemed reasonable:

> I began to realize that I believed countless things which I had never seen or which had taken place when I was not there to see. . . . Most of all it came home to me how firm and unshakeable was the faith which told me who my parents were, because I never could have known this unless I believed what I was told. In this way you [God] made me understand that I ought not to find fault with those who believed your Bible, which you have established with such great authority amongst almost all the nations of the earth.[23]

Augustine had come a long way, yet he confessed, "I kept delaying my conversion to you, my God. Day after day I postponed living in you. . . . I longed for a life of happiness but I was frightened to approach it in its own domain; and yet, while I fled from it, I still searched for it."[24] And the cause of his being obstructed thus?: "I thought it would be too much for me to bear if I were to be deprived of woman's love." But matters were to be expedited as the mistress, with whom he had lived for years and who had borne him a son, left him and the child, and returned home to North Africa. He had previously contracted an agreement whereby two years thence he was to be married; but, in the meantime, he was incapable of continence, so he took another mistress, admitting that he "was more a slave of lust than a true lover of marriage."[25]

After a further period of procrastination, and consequent frustration, Augustine found himself in a narrow, and increasingly constricted path whose goal was humanly unattainable:

> In my heart I kept saying "Let it be now, let it be now!", and merely saying this I was on the point of making the resolution. I was on the point of making it, but I did not succeed. Yet I did not fall back into my old state. I stood on the brink of resolution, waiting to take fresh breath. I tried again and came a little nearer to my goal, and then a little nearer still, so that I could almost reach out and grasp it. But I did not reach it.

[23]Ibid.

[24]Ibid., 128.

[25]Ibid., 131.

I could not reach out to it or grasp it, because I held back from the step
by which I should die to death and become alive to life. My lower in-
stincts, which had taken firm hold of me, were stronger than the higher,
which were untried. And the closer I came to the moment which was to
mark the great change in me, the more I shrank from it in horror. But it
did not drive me back or turn me from my purpose: it merely left me
hanging in suspense.[26]

Then one day, mercifully, he reached the end of himself: "I felt that
I was still the captive of my sins, and in my misery I kept crying 'How long
shall I go on saying "tomorrow, tomorrow"'? Why not now? Why not make
an end of my ugly sins at this moment?' "[27] Reason was no longer a consideration— unless he was touched by some power outside himself his quest
for Truth was at a standstill, and he, himself, undone.

I was asking myself these questions, weeping all the while with the most
bitter sorrow in my heart, when all at once I heard the singsong voice of
a child in a nearby house. Whether it was the voice of a boy or a girl I
cannot say, but again and again it repeated the refrain "Take it and read,
take it and read." At this I looked up, thinking hard whether there was
any kind of game in which children used to chant words like these, but I
could not remember ever hearing them before. I stemmed my flood of
tears and stood up, telling myself that this could only be a divine com-
mand to open my book of Scripture and read the first passage on which
my eyes should fall. . . . I hurried back to the place where Alypius was
sitting, for when I stood up to move away I had put down the book containing Paul's Epistles. I seized it and opened it, and in silence read the
first passage on which my eyes fell: *Not in revelling and drunkenness,
not in lust and wantonness, not in quarrels and rivalries. Rather, arm
yourselves with the Lord Jesus Christ; spend no more thought on nature
and nature's appetites.* I had no wish to read more and no need to do
so. For in an instant as I came to the end of the sentence, it was as though
the light of confidence flooded into my heart and all the darkness of doubt
was dispelled.*[28]

---

[26]Ibid., 175.

[27]Ibid., 177.

*Romans 13:13-14.

[28]Augustine, *Confessions*, 177, 178.

It is remarkable what power is conveyed by the simplest passage of Scripture to the soul ready to receive life from above.

It is most important to observe that Augustine did not here "have a change of mind," "turn over a new leaf," or even "make the leap of faith."† Something *happened to him* which opened up another dimension. Jesus told Nicodemus, "Except a man be born from above he cannot see the kingdom of God. . . . Except a man be born of water and the Spirit he cannot enter into the kingdom of God (Jn 3:3-5)." Augustine went to the Word of God (the water) and encountered the Spirit who breathed spiritual life into him. This was the same spiritual crisis as for Paul on the Damascus road—but with a difference. Whereas immediately before his spiritual crisis Paul was running blindly counter to Christ spiritually, intellectually, rationally and naturally, and was arrested in his tracks experiencing a total reversal, Augustine experienced a rational reorientation and was intellectually convinced of the rightness of the Gospel some time before his spiritual conversion.

In his introduction to Trotter's English translation of Pascal's *Pensées,* T. S. Eliot describes what he regards as the process of the mind of the intelligent believer.

> The Christian thinker—and I mean the man who is trying consciously and conscientiously to explain to himself the sequence which culminated in faith, rather than the public apologist—proceeds by rejection and elimination. He finds the world to be so and so; he finds its character inexplicable by any non-religious theory; among religions he finds Christianity, and Catholic Christianity, to account most satisfactorily for the world and especially for the moral world within; and thus, by what Newman calls "powerful and concurrent" reasons, he finds himself inexorably committed to the dogma of the Incarnation.[29]

Augustine would consent, to a degree, that this was the way he went, but he would have at least two observations: (1) T. S. Eliot's process does not mention the inner reorientation whereby the reason becomes no longer hostile to faith but sympathetic to it (but perhaps T. S. Eliot regards this

---

†For a full discussion of the "leap of faith" see the chapter bearing that title in my *The Spiritual Quest of Albert Camus* (Tuscaloosa AL: Portals Press, 1976).

[29]Blaise Pascal, *Pensées,* trans. W. F. Trotter, Everyman's Library (New York: E. P. Dutton and Co., 1932) xii.

crisis as the starting point of his process); and (2) the Key—being spiritually reborn from above, without which there is nothing conclusive and substantial—is absent.

The principal question is whether there is such a thing as intellectual progression towards conversion, or whether the nature of the intellectual activity is simply symptomatic of the heart attitude which latter has to reach a certain condition before there can be spiritual rebirth from above. Augustine, I believe, would have held that the latter is the truth; and yet, after his conversion, he was lured, not infrequently, into using his naked reason in his efforts to establish or develop the purposes of God—a carry over from the past, the habit of a brilliant intellect trained in rhetoric and logic.

Watchman Nee, the well-known Chinese Christian who died in 1972, tells a fascinating anecdote. In college he was friendly with a highly intelligent young man who went on to become a prominent philosopher. Watchman Nee travelled throughout China preaching the Gospel and establishing local Christian gatherings. His journeys led him to the city where this young philosopher was a college professor, so he went to visit him. The conversation was brief, the philosopher protesting that, enlightened as he was by his philosophy, he could not possibly believe in the resurrection of Christ. Watchman Nee apparently said to him such words as, "You should tell that, not to me, but to the Lord, and see what He will say." The philosopher evidently appeared at the meetings at which Watchman Nee was speaking, and, in a few days, was spiritually reborn from above. It was doubtless Watchman Nee's refusal to engage in rational disputation which expedited this philosopher's entry into the kingdom.

THOMAS AQUINAS

Towards the end of his forty-eighth year, in early December 1273, Thomas Aquinas had what Anthony Kenny calls a "mysterious experience" while saying Mass, following which he never again wrote or dictated anything. When his secretary, Brother Reginald, begged him to continue his work on the almost completed *Summa theologica,* he simply replied, "I cannot, because all that I have written now seems like straw." When, a little later, Brother Reginald repeated the plea, Aquinas replied more explicitly, "Everything that I have written seems to me as worthless in comparison with the things I have seen and which have been revealed to me."[30] Some interpret this "mysterious experience" as a mental break-

[30]Anthony Kenny, *Aquinas* (New York: Hill and Wang, 1980) 26.

down whereas others call it a vision. There is evidence, I believe, both in these statements and in what transpired at that time and shortly after, that it was not the former, and was indeed the latter.

Early the following year, 1274, Pope Gregory X called for a general council of the Church at Lyons. The main topic was to be the reconciliation between the Greek and Latin Churches. Aquinas was summoned to attend in his capacity as an expert on Greek Theology. He was not well physically when he set out for Lyons, and suffered an accidental head injury en route (his head struck a branch overhanging the road) forcing him to take shelter in a neighboring castle owned by his niece. After a few weeks he was conveyed to a nearby Cistercian monastery at Fossanova where he died in early March 1274, just four months after the "experience." His death was surprising because, though he had seemed preoccupied and a little out of sorts during the preceding few months, he was normally a vigorous man and the accidental head injury is not regarded as having been very serious. "The sources never give an adequate reason for his death," observed Vernon Bourke.[31]

Had Aquinas suffered a nervous breakdown, as some suggest, his behavior would have been characterized by disorder, disorientation, distress, or delusions, none of which appear in either of the statements cited above. The apostle Paul could equally well have uttered these words at his conversion, the only difference being that, in his case, what he was leaving behind was not intellectual Christianity but Judaism. Indeed, when Paul testified before Agrippa and Festus concerning the crisis of "the heavenly vision" (Acts 26:19) in his life, Festus thought he had gone out of his mind: "Paul, thou art mad; thy much learning hath turned thee to madness" (Acts 26:24). There are likewise those who attribute Aquinas's "mysterious experience" to madness brought on by much learning.

But the thrust of the two statements is wholly positive. Aquinas had "seen" some things he had never seen before, and these things had been "revealed" to him. By comparison, everything he had ever written paled into insignificance, seeming "worthless" as so much "straw." Four months following "the experience" he was dead. There seems no accounting for so sudden, unexpected, and premature a death.

The learned Alexandrian Apollos, who had been taught by word of

---

[31]Vernon Bourke, *Aquinas's search for Wisdom* (Milwaukee: Bruce Pub. Co., 1965) 194.

mouth and was fervent in spirit, went to Ephesus where he "spake and taught carefully the things concerning Jesus, knowing only the baptism of John" (Acts 18:25). Priscilla and Aquila heard him and took him aside and "expounded unto him the way of God more carefully" (Acts 18:26), but his ministry had already brought into being a group who were later to say to Paul, who had sensed something lacking in them, "We did not so much as hear whether there is a Holy Ghost" (Acts 19:2). It was impossible for Apollos to stay in Ephesus. He might have been able to return after a suitable lapse of time; but he could not expect those who had been converted through his message to be able to accept at once such a radical difference in teaching through him—it would have to come through some other servant whom God would send, or through Priscilla or Aquila. So, encouraged by the brethren at Ephesus who wrote ahead to recommend him, he sailed over to Achaia, to fresh ground, armed with a new and complete Gospel, and was mightily used by God.

But Aquinas's teaching was not just to one city: in his lifetime it spread throughout Christendom, and he must have sensed that the corpus of his written material was to play a vital and fundamental role in the doctrine of the whole Catholic Church. The world was too small for him; there was no place to which he could go and start afresh. It is probable also that he felt he could not speak openly of the revelations he had received for fear of the disruptions it might cause. This would explain why, when he made the second of the above statements to Brother Reginald, he prefaced it by saying, "I adjure you by the living and omnipotent God, by the loyalty you have for the Order, and by the charity that binds us together, to tell nothing during my lifetime of what I reveal to you."[32]

It is recorded that, as he entered the Cistercian monastery at Fossanova, Aquinas said, "This is my rest for ever and ever . . ." (a quotation from Psalm 131:14). His physical condition deteriorated further but he suffered his illness with great patience:

> Before receiving the Body of Christ, he spoke many fitting words concerning the Body of Christ in the presence of the whole congregation of monks of the said monastery and of many from the Order of Preachers and of Minors [Franciscans]. In the midst of this discourse, he uttered these words, "I have taught and written a great deal about this most holy Body and the other sacraments, in the faith of Christ and the holy Roman

[32]Ibid., 193.

Church, to whose correction I submit and leave it all." Then having received this Body, he lived for three days and on the third day he slept in the Lord.[33]

In his last recorded statement Aquinas was still preoccupied and burdened with what he had taught and written: he suggests and invites its correction. As in the case of Apollos, he would have to leave the righting of the theological ship to someone or ones who would follow him. Yet all the evidence points to Aquinas's leaving this life a man at peace with his Lord and Savior. No sign of mental derangement here. In Mercy, God took him.

It was probably during the year 1225 A.D. that Thomas Aquinas was born into the aristocratic feudal house of Aquino whose principal residence was the castle of Roccasecca near Naples. When he was just five years old his father sent him to be educated at the great Benedictine abbey at Monte Cassino, about halfway between Naples and Rome. It is uncertain whether he was enrolled as a lay student or as an oblate (not quite a child monk, but with greater expectation of monastic commitment than a modern schoolboy at a Benedictine preparatory school)[34]—the latter is more likely as it is later recorded that his parents hoped their son would one day become the abbot of Monte Cassino.

If our morals are no better, our wisdom no wiser than in those days, at least we have learned some things about the impressionability of childhood and youth. The Lord Jesus' prayer on our behalf is clear: "I pray not that thou [God] shouldest take them out of the world, but that thou shouldest keep them from the evil one" (Jn 17:15). Being in the world is thus normal, whereas the monastic life abstracts from "the world," its motive being to "protect from" with a view to facilitating "devotion to"—but that devotion must be abnormal in manifestation, living and drawing its sustenance from a rarefied, anomalous context.

What I have just said would seem to be confirmed by an incident in Thomas's life which followed his early education at Monte Cassino, five years at the Imperial University at Naples and his decision to become a Dominican friar. (The Dominicans combine a life of poverty and obedience with devotion to scholarship and evangelical zeal.) Thomas's zeal propel-

---

[33]Ibid., 212.

[34]Kenny, *Aquinas*, 1.

led him outside his family's expectations; they saw their ambition of his becoming abbot of Monte Cassino dashed to the ground, and decided to do all they could to force him back on the former track. His natural brothers waylaid him one day, while he was journeying on foot, and tried to persuade him to remove his Dominican habit. When he refused they literally kidnapped him and took him back to the family castle at Montesangiovanni where they detained him for a period of at least a few months, and possibly, according to some biographers, up to two years. It is likely that, for the latter part of his confinement, he was brought to the principal family residence at Roccasecca.

During this period the family used every means available to try to persuade Thomas to break his resolution and leave the Dominican order. There is one surprising incident which shows how far they were prepared to go

> While he [Thomas] was alone in the room in which he customarily slept under custody, they sent in a very attractive girl decked out like a prostitute. She tempted him to sin, using all the devices at her disposal, glances, caresses and gestures. The fighter [Thomas] had taken God's wisdom as his spouse and beloved, and he was not overcome by her appearance. Yet when he began to feel fleshly desire rise within him, which he always had kept under rational control (this exception was allowed by consent of divine providence, so that he might rise to a more glorious triumph from this test), he snatched a burning stick from the fireplace and indignantly chased the girl out of his room.
>
> Internally raging, he strode to a corner of the room, made the sign of the cross on the wall with the point of the burning stick and, prostrating himself tearfully on the floor, prayerfully begged God for the girdle of perpetual virginity to keep himself immaculate in temptation. While praying and in tears, he suddenly fell asleep. Behold, two angels were sent to him from heaven: they told him that he had been heard by God and that he had gained a triumph in a very difficult struggle. Binding him tightly about the loins, they said: "See how, acting on God's behalf, we bind you with the belt of chastity, as you have asked, and it cannot be broken in any temptation. This gift which cannot be gained from the merits of human virtue is granted to you out of divine liberality."[35]

That this account by William of Tocco is imaginative, at least in part, can be seen from the actual outcome. Aquinas's earliest biographer says

---

[35]Bourke, *Aquinas's search for Wisdom*, 37.

that "from that time onwards it was his custom always to avoid the sight and company of women—except in case of necessity or utility—as a man avoids snakes."[36] Such a defensive, fearful attitude hardly corresponds with the gift of the belt of chastity, granted out of divine liberality, which was supposedly impregnable in any temptation. Nor is it fitting testimony to a "more glorious triumph" to which he had supposedly risen from this test. None of this is intended in judgment of Thomas—he was as human as any. We should never lose sight of the fact that there was a group of devout women in almost constant attendance upon the Lord Jesus and His disciples (Lk 8:1-3), and it was almost certainly women, Mary and Martha, who, during His lifetime upon this earth, understood Him and His purposes best, and with whom He could converse most deeply (Jn 11:1–12:8). He did not have to be defensive in their presence as if they were snakes.

What, one might ask, would Augustine have to say concerning all this? He, for whom inability to live a life of continence was the very issue which drove him first to despair in himself, and thence to being spiritually reborn from above. One cannot subscribe to the convenient self-serving doctrine of "Shall we continue in sin, that grace may abound? . . . Shall we sin, because we are not under law, but under grace" (Rom 6:1, 15). Yet it is inescapable that the grace of God is revealed against the backdrop of the weakness and sin of man. The Lord Jesus explained to a Pharisee that gratitude is proportionate to the size of the debt forgiven (Lk 7:47). The debt is usually first felt as a consequence of acts—sins— committed; and not, unfortunately, as acutely from a perception of the innate sinfulness of human nature. The Pharisee is wide awake to the former—sinful acts incurring guilt—and follows the law to seek to avoid them; but, as to himself, he is almost totally unconscious of the latter—the inner sinful nature which is the common lot of all men. As a consequence of his life "in the world," Augustine reached the point where he knew he had a deep need of forgiveness, and was powerless to live as he would; but Aquinas, at the tender age of five, was cloistered and protected, until he was about fourteen, in an atmosphere in which everything was designed to insulate him from the world, and to teach him to be strong in himself.

Thomas's very nature, taciturn and tending towards solitude and meditation, suited him for this life. From the beginning, his was a philosophic and intellectual turn of mind—it is recorded that, as a child at Monte Cas-

---

[36]Kenny, *Aquinas,* 2.

sino, he often asked the question, "What is God?" and then committed
the answer to memory. From Monte Cassino he went to the Imperial University at Naples where, until he was nineteen, he studied particularly the
philosophy of Aristotle. The next seven years were spent in Paris and Col-
ogne studying theology and, again, Aristotle, under Albert the Great who
was "the first Dominican scholar to attempt to utilize all of the philosophy
of Aristotle in the service of Christian Theology."[37] It is little wonder, that,
as Aristotelianism grew to be "the most important element in Thomism
(the theological doctrine of Thomas Aquinas),"[38] it became fashionable to
say that Thomas Aquinas "baptized Aristotle."

Aquinas's capacity for work was extraordinary. He produced the "Se-
cunda Pars," more than a million words long, in three years, averaging
about a thousand words a day. His chief secretary attests that it was his
custom, like the grand master in a chess tournament, to dictate to three or
four secretaries simultaneously.[39] Yet Aquinas said that all he had written
seemed to him like "straw" after his mysterious experience. He did not
say that it seemed wrong, or incorrect, but like "straw"—lifeless, and thus
worthless.

To illustrate my thesis, passages from Augustine and Aquinas are included below, in appendix A. I have selected from Aquinas that work
which, from its title, appeared most likely to breathe spiritual life. I chose
his *Meditations,* and from them *The Greatness of Divine Love*—a commentary on the well-known sixteenth verse of the third chapter of John's
Gospel: "God so loved the world, that he gave his only begotten Son; that
whosoever believeth on him should not perish, but have eternal life." I
suggest that what Aquinas says is true, correct, and perceptive, yet somehow dry, lacking an element which one expects this verse to evoke from a
consciously redeemed man. It is as if it was composed dispassionately—
the thing written savoring more of philosophic deduction than of authori-
tative fruit of scriptural truth experienced personally.

In their *Augustine and Thomas Aquinas,* Norman Cantor and Peter
Klein ask, "Why did Christian theorists devote considerable time and effort to the work of Plato and Aristotle whose teachings often conflicted with

[37]Bourke, *Aquinas's search for Wisdom,* 47.

[38]Ibid., 73.

[39]Kenny, *Aquinas,* 25.

the dogmas of the Christian faith?'' Then they answer their own question: ''The reason is simply that not only did Greek philosophy function as a catalyst for medieval thought, but, from the Greeks, Christian thinkers acquired the language and method of philosophical enquiry. Using these tools for their own purpose, medieval theorists fashioned an original Christian philosophy.''[40] Therein lies the difficulty. I quote again what Camus writes on this subject: ''When it first appears, Christianity is not a philosophy, but a harmonious set of aspirations, a faith, which operates within a certain context and seeks its answers within that context.''[41] It was the scholastics of the Middle Ages who invented this monstrosity which, in the mercy of God, the church survived, as attested by the fact that, while scholars may range more widely in plying their trade, Christians today read only the truly spiritual works of Augustine—the *Confessions* and *The City of God*—and little at all by Aquinas.

---

[40]Norman Cantor and Peter Klein, *Augustine and Thomas Aquinas* (Waltham MA: Blaisdell Pub. Co., 1969) 1.

[41]Albert Camus, *Essais,* Bibliothèque de la Pléiade (Paris: Éditions Gallimard, 1965) 1224 (A.T.).

CHAPTER 3

The Mystics

———— // ————

Most frequently it [mysticism] appears historically, in relation to some definite system of belief, as a reaction of the spirit against the letter. When a religion begins to ossify into a system of formulas and observances, those who protest in the name of heart-religion are not infrequently known by the name of mystics. . . . Mysticism first appears in the medieval Church as the protest of practical religion against the predominance of the dialectical spirit. [1]

Today's quest for the charismatic experience, in reaction to the deadness of many Christian institutions, corresponds to the deliberate movement of the mystics away from the desiccating influence of Scholasticism. The mystics and the charismatics are akin to one another—each seeks, and believes to experience, sensory manifestations of his union with God; manifestations which comfort by evidencing experientially God's goodness towards man.

Even as scholasticism was the fruit of a misguided attempt to express Christian truths in "metaphysical formulae which it found ready-made" [2] by adopting the forms of Greek thought, so mysticism also has Greek

---

[1] *Encyclopaedia Britannica,* 1957 edition, 16:51.

[2] Albert Camus, *Essais,* Bibliothèque de la Pléide (Paris: Éditions Gallimard, 1965) 1224 (A.T.).

origins in Plato, and his idealism. It was developed through Plotinus. But whereas to Plato "The One," the Good, and the notion or idea of God were all one entity, Plotinus developed the thesis of distinction between "the One" and what he called the *nous*— "the One" being above existence itself, according to him, and incomprehensible to reason, whereas the *nous* was a sort of formless intuition in which was manifested the whole nature of the Absolute.[3]

> Remaining itself in repose, it [the One] rays out, as it were, from its own fullness an image of itself, which is called *nous,* and which constitutes the system of ideas of the intelligible world. The soul is in turn the image or product of the *nous,* and the soul by its motion begets corporeal matter. The soul thus faces two ways—towards the *nous,* from which it springs, and towards the material life, which is its own product. Ethical endeavour consists in the repudiation of the sensible; material existence is itself estrangement from God. (Porphyry tells us that Plotinus was unwilling to name his parents or his birthplace, and seemed ashamed of being in the body.) . . . To reach the ultimate goal, thought itself must be left behind; for thought is a form of motion, and the desire of the soul is for the motionless rest which belongs to the One. The union with transcendent deity is not so much knowledge or vision as ecstasy, coalescence, *contact.* . . . But in our present state of existence the moments of this ecstatic union must be few and far apart.[4]

Now Plotinus's position is a philosophic theory which is easily and fully comprehensible rationally. The theory teaches the would-be initiate, however, that his reason, by which he grasped the theory, is useless in his quest for God—it thus invites mysticism, a turning away from the body and rational thought, and a voluntary surrender, an opening up of the self to receive the *nous* from the One and only, and otherwise intangible, supreme being. On the surface it appears that Plotinus's notion of man—a trichotomy of *nous,* soul and body—is very similar to that of the New Testament—spirit, soul and body—but the difference is basic, and has far reaching consequences.

---

[3]*Encyclopaedia Britannica,* 1957 edition, 18:82.

[4]Ibid., 16:51.

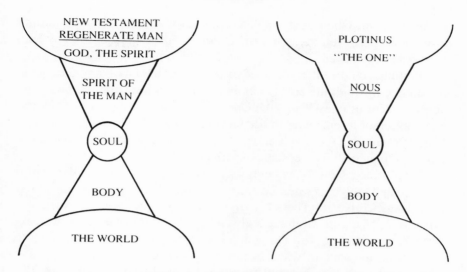

NEW TESTAMENT
REGENERATE MAN
GOD, THE SPIRIT
SPIRIT OF
THE MAN
SOUL
BODY
THE WORLD

PLOTINUS
"THE ONE"
NOUS
SOUL
BODY
THE WORLD

The New Testament teaches that man (all parts of him—body, soul and spirit) is fallen and shut out of God's presence, but that "whensoever a man shall turn to the Lord, the veil is taken away" (2 Cor 3:16; see diagrams in chapter 1, above). Until this crisis, a man may register the Holy Spirit's impress on his spirit from time to time, but he will not allow it to govern—in the final analysis it will always be his soul, his own will and mind, which predominates. Sometimes, if the Holy Spirit's touch produces sufficient discomfort, an unredeemed person may choose to give in to it for a time or over some issue, for the sake of peace, and then revert later to his former position of authority--occasionally conceding a momentary battle; but never losing the war. The crisis is "whensoever a man shall turn to the Lord": when he deliberately turns from his own will and mind, and submits himself in obedience to the Lord through his spirit ("the spirit of the man which is in him," 1 Cor 2:11). After this initial crisis, life becomes a series of crises, sometime minor and sometimes major, and the issue at each one is spiritual obedience. As already described in chapter 1, each act of obedience brings further revelation of spiritual reality, and from this there springs deeper wisdom and spiritual perception which "focussing into an attitude and outlook, could be called the *nous*" (see above, p. 8). It should be noted here that even the Lord Jesus went this way— there was no original sin in Him, of course, but He nevertheless "learned obedience by the things which He suffered" (Heb 5:8), "becoming obedient even unto death" (Phil 2:8). Even for Him obedience was *learned*; He *be-*

came obedient. Obedience is a deep well, each crisis leading to a further test at a deeper level, and it has to be *learned,* experienced, even by Him who never disobeyed.

Plotinus, on the other hand, advocates, not a submission of the soul in obedience through the spirit, but an ascetic turning from the body and abandonment of oneself to ''the One'' from whom the *nous* (his, Plotinus's, notion of it) emanates to become the source of a new life for the soul which growingly finds itself at one with the transcendent deity; and all of this to be punctuated by ecstatic experiences.

The former, New Testament, way has as its objective that the ''spirit and soul and body be preserved entire, without blame at the coming of our Lord Jesus Christ'' (1 Thess 5:23), whereas the latter seeks, in monastic separation, an escape from the body and the world into a metaphysical experience of merging with the deity. The former is advanced by death to self, losing the soul—''whosoever would save his soul shall lose it: and whosoever shall lose his soul for my sake shall find it'' (Matt 16:25); whereas the latter seeks to lose the body. The former speaks of a healthy normal spirituality, recognizable by anyone; but the latter speaks of ethereality, something apart, and abnormally supernatural.

Rudolph Eucken, a German philosopher of the late nineteenth and early twentieth centuries, estimates that the non-Christian Plotinus had a greater impact upon Christian thought than any other person, Christian or non-Christian. Ernst Troeltsch, also German and a contemporary of Rudolf Eucken, contends that the Catholic Church does not belong to the Middle Ages but is rather the last creative effort of classical antiquity, which may be said to have died in giving birth to it.[5] Centuries before scholasticism reached its peak and muddied the briefly clear waters, mysticism had already infiltrated the Church; but there it waited, only later to grow and take definite form as a reaction to the arid logic of the scholastics.

It is no doubt advisedly that the Lord likens His people to sheep. There are the true ones who hear His voice and follow Him (Jn 10:4) in their quest for truth and sanctification. Yet the great majority in any age follow the current vogue. Thus it is that most of the Christian mystics, who are not numerous, became such as a result of their dissatisfaction with the prevailing spiritual climate, and, if they did allow the swing of the pendulum to carry them past dead center, it was in reaction to what they knew to be

---

[5]Ibid., 18:81.

less than pleasing to the Lord. In the case of many of them their writings are for the most part pure and spiritual, with only an occasional lapse into mysticism. Thomas à Kempis is an excellent example.

Thomas à Kempis—so named after his birthplace, Kempen, near Düsseldorf in Germany—was the second son of humble parents of whom little is known. His elder brother John, born in 1365, left home and attached himself to the "Congregation of the Common Life," a brotherhood at Deventer in the Netherlands, founded by the great spiritual reformer Gerard Groote. Here Thomas (born in 1379/1380) joined his brother when he was but thirteen years old.

Gerald Groote died of the plague in 1384 at which time the responsibility for the direction of the brotherhood passed to Florentius Radewyns who acted as Thomas's spiritual guide during his first six years of monastic life. In 1399, with the approval of Radewyns, Thomas travelled the twenty or so miles north to Windesheim, near Zwolle, where his brother John had assumed the priorship of the new monastery of Mount St. Agnes. Here Thomas lived a quiet and outwardly uneventful life until his death at the ripe old age of ninety-two. He had made his profession at the age of twenty-six, and entered the priesthood when he was thirty-three. He wrote a good number of devotional works on the spiritual life and several biographies, including those of Groote and Radewyns. The work for which he has become famous, and which continues to be as popular today as ever, is his *De imitatione Christi, The Imitation of Christ.*

After all that has been said here regarding mysticism being a reaction to scholasticism, it is not surprising to find numerous passages in *The Imitation of Christ,* particularly in the early pages, that warn against supposing that human intellect, on its own, can successfully penetrate to the meaning of the things of God. Thomas sounds this warning on the very first page, beginning about the fourteenth line of the text:

> Of what use is it to discourse learnedly on the Trinity, if you lack humility and therefore displease the Trinity? Lofty words do not make a man just or holy; but a good life makes him dear to God. I would far rather feel contrition than be able to define it. If you knew the whole Bible by heart, and all the teachings of the philosophers, how would this help you without the grace and love of God.[6]

---

[6]Thomas à Kempis, *The Imitation of Christ,* trans. Leo Sherley-Price, Classics Series (New York: Penguin Books, 1952) 27.

Then Thomas's second chapter begins with

> Everyone naturally desires knowledge, but of what use is knowledge
> without the fear of God? A humble countryman who serves God is more
> pleasing to Him than a conceited intellectual who knows the course of
> the stars.[7]

Thomas's chapter 3, "On the Teaching of Truth," is devoted almost entirely to this subject, as suggested by the following excerpt.

> Of what value are lengthy controversies on deep and obscure matters,
> when it is not by our knowledge of such matters that we shall at length
> be judged. . . . Often I am wearied by all I read and hear. In You [God]
> alone is all that I desire and long for. Therefore let all teachers keep si-
> lence, and let all creation be still before You; do You, O Lord, speak
> alone. . . . But because many are more eager to acquire much learning
> than to live well, they often go astray, and bear little or no fruit. . . . Tell
> me, where are now all those Masters and Doctors whom you knew so
> well in their lifetime in the full flower of their learning? Other men now
> sit in their seats, and they are hardly ever called to mind. In their lifetime
> they seemed of great account, but now no one speaks of them.[8]

Chapter 5 of *The Imitation of Christ* deals with the reading of "holy writings":

> In them ["holy writings"], therefore, we should seek food for our souls
> rather than subtleties of speech, and we should as readily read simple and
> devout books as those that are lofty and profound.[9]

Later, in book 3, chapter 31, Thomas summarizes:

> There is a great difference between the wisdom of a devout man en-
> lightened by God, and the knowledge of a learned and studious scholar.
> More noble by far is the learning infused from above by divine grace,
> than that painfully acquired by the industry of man.[10]

---

[7]Ibid., 28.

[8]Ibid., 30-31.

[9]Ibid., 33.

[10]Ibid., 136.

The seclusion of the monastic life is the first practical step in the mystic's quest for spiritual release through physical separation and solitude; this was the way espoused by Thomas à Kempis. Thus it is no wonder that, at the other end of the spectrum in *The Imitation of Christ,* there are occasional indications of the mystic's longing for an escape from this world and a merging with God.

> A wise man once said "As often as I have been among men, I have returned home a lesser man." We often share this experience, when we spend much time in conversation. It is easier to keep silence altogether than not to talk more than we should. It is easier to remain quietly at home than to keep due watch over ourselves in public. Therefore, whoever is resolved to live an inward and spiritual life must, with Jesus, withdraw from the crowd.[11]

While it is true that Jesus withdrew for times of prayer and communion with His Father, yet, during the three years of His ministry, was ever a man more public, more often engaged in serious conversation, more constantly under scrutiny from all sides, more available, than He? "It is commendable in a Religious [that is, here, a monastic]," Thomas advised, "to go abroad but seldom, to avoid being seen, and to have no desire to see men."[12] Here one can see a certain spiritual exclusiveness never even hinted at in Jesus Christ. Monastic seclusion produces an aloof, ethereal form of spirituality. How much more meaningful and robust is that spirituality that grows from service among men, with all the sensitivity to others, patience and long suffering that this demands.

There are occasional passages in *The Imitation of Christ* that almost savor of Plotinus's escape into the ecstatic experience of merging into "The One."

> O Lord Jesus Christ, spouse of the soul, lover of purity, and Lord of creation, who will give me the wings of perfect liberty, that I may fly to You, and be at rest? When shall I become recollected in You, that for the love of You I may no longer be conscious of myself, but of You alone in a manner not known to all men, and above all perception and measure?[13]

---

[11]Ibid., 50.

[12]Ibid., 52.

[13]Ibid., 121.

In book 3 of *The Imitation*— ''On Inward Consolation'' (or ''Of Inner Comfort'')—Thomas writes in the form of a dialogue between Christ and a disciple.

> CHRIST. My son, My grace is precious, and may not be mingled with worldly concerns and pleasures. Therefore, if you wish to receive it, you must remove every obstacle to grace. Seek out a place apart, and love the solitary life. Do not engage in conversation with men, but instead pour forth devout prayer to God, that you may preserve a humble mind and a clean conscience. . . . Remain detached from acquaintances and friends and independent of this world's consolations.[14]

Yet, in between the indictment of the scholastic's rationalized Christianity and brief sallies into mysticism, there is a wealth of spiritual instruction and exhortation in *The Imitation of Christ,* with a strong emphasis on obedience, for which this work has justifiably become, and remains, universally popular.

> Can one distil from religious or mystical experience certain pure elements which are common everywhere in all religions? . . . If a Christian mystic has an experience which can be phenomenologically compared with a Zen experience, does it matter that the Christian in fact believes that he is personally united with God and the Zen man interprets his experience as *Sunyata* or the Void being aware of itself?[15]

So wrote Thomas Merton, the famous Christian poet and mystic who, during the latter part of his life, lived in the Trappist monastery of Gethsemane near Bardstown, Kentucky. Two years after writing this Merton was dead, accidentally electrocuted while journeying in the East in his quest to discover if there were in fact any differences in the meditation techniques used by Buddhist and Hindu mystics in the East and those used by Christian mystics in the West: he concluded there are none.

> It is never easy to say with any security that what a Christian mystic and Sufi [Islamic mystic] and Zen Master experience is really ''the same thing.'' But there are nevertheless certain analogies and correspondence which are evident even now, and which may perhaps point out the way

---

[14]Ibid., 167.

[15]C. H. W. John, *The Golden Age of Zen,* intro. by Thomas Merton (National War College, 1967) 11.

to a better mutual understanding. . . . Now in Zen, what is communicated is not a message. It is not simply a ''word,'' even though it might be the ''word of the Lord.'' It is not a ''what.'' It does not bring ''news'' which the receiver did not already have, about something the one informed did not yet know. What Zen communicates is an awareness that is potentially already there but is not conscious of itself. Zen is then not Kerygma* but realization, not revelation but consciousness, not news from the Father who sends His Son into this world, but awareness of the ontological ground of our own being here and now, right in the midst of the world. We will see later that the supernatural Kerygma and the metaphysical intuition of the ground of being are far from being incompatible. One may be said to prepare the way for the other. They can well complement each other, and for this reason Zen is perfectly compatible with Christian belief and indeed with Christian mysticism (if we understand Zen in its pure state, as metaphysical intuition).[16]

At first Merton seemed unsure, as if there were as yet insufficient evidence to prove any kinship between the experience of the Christian mystic and the man of Zen. But, in this latter quotation, he grows bold and claims that the two are ''perfectly compatible'' provided we understand Zen in its pure state, as a metaphysical intuition. In this Merton was somewhat in advance of his fellow Christian mystics who still regarded it essential for ''the Christ of faith to be present as ikon at the center of Christian contemplation.''[17] But, with ecumenism spreading, and the centrality of the Cross of Jesus Christ being de-emphasized to give the occasion for world religions to flow together,† Thomas Merton will be found to have been prophetic.

Man is far more complex than generally thought; he has extraordinary psychic powers which enable him, through the practice of certain meditation techniques to reach a heightened awareness, an impression of illumination, and an apparent merging with a transcendental power—all of which is beyond common everyday experience and has to be induced, but is not Christian. A Christian may also practice mysticism (if he does, his

---

*Greek κήρυγμα *kerygma* = what is preached, message, proclamation.

[16]John, *The Golden Age of Zen,* 12, 15, and 16.

[17]Ibid., 13.

†See chap. 3, ''Religion—The World's Religions—Mystery Babylon the Great,'' of my book *He Is Nigh* (Tuscaloosa AL: Portals Press, 1980).

perception of spiritual principles will become less clear), but there is no mysticism in true Christianity. The mystic seeks a sensory experience; whereas the spiritual Christian seeks sanctification—that is, permanent character change. The mystic reaches for the ecstasy and rapture of a metaphysical encounter, which will be fleeting; the obedient Christian is rewarded with peace "which passeth all understanding" (Phil 4:7) as the common denominator to all of life's experience.

CHAPTER 4

Montaigne

—————— // ——————

Michel Eyquem de Montaigne was born 28 February 1533. His father, a soldier and lawyer, was also a well-to-do landowner in Bordeaux and in the nearby Dordogne valley where the property bore the family name (Château de Montaigne).

Soon after his birth, Michel was passed to the care of a peasant nurse; then, before he learned to talk, his father entrusted him to a German tutor who was totally ignorant of French but well versed in Latin.

> This man . . . carried me around constantly; and with him he had two others less learned, to look after me and relieve him. None of them spoke to me in any language but Latin. . . . I learnt Latin as pure as my master's own, for I had no way of adulterating or confusing it.[1]

At about age six the young boy was sent to the College of Guienne where his Latin was useful but soon corrupted. At age thirteen he left this school and went for a time to the University of Bordeaux whence he transferred to the University of Toulouse when he was sixteen to be trained in law. He held a legal post at Périgueux for two or three years, then, in 1557, returned to Bordeaux where his father was then mayor.

In 1561 he was sent on a mission to the Royal Court in Paris; two years

---

[1]Michel de Montaigne, *Essays*, trans. Donald M. Frame, Classics Series (repr. Baltimore MD: Penguin, 1958) 81.

later he returned to work in the courts at Bordeaux. In 1565 he married a wealthy heiress; three years later his father died, leaving him the family estate of Montaigne. When he was thirty-eight he returned to this Château de Montaigne in the Dordogne valley, and here, apart from journeys he made seeking a cure for kidney stones from which he suffered, and a relatively brief period as mayor of Bordeaux, he spent the rest of his life in leisurely fashion, caring for his property, meditating in his well-stocked library, and writing. His one collection of writings (other than his journal and letters), frequently revised and elaborated with additional annotations, eventually became three "books" entitled *Essais* (*Essays*).

Montaigne coined (literally—he had a medal struck) a dictum which has become his hallmark, and which betrays the thrust of his thought: "Que sais-je?" ("What do I know?"). But the more one reads Montaigne, particularly his most important philosophical work, "In Defense of Raimond Sebond," the more one feels he was really asking, "Is it possible for me to be sure I know anything?"* He was convinced that it was presumptuous on the part of man to think he could know all about and really understand anything: God alone was capable of that. He was "persuaded that everything had already been thought and said, and was anxious to show that man is always and everywhere one and the same."[2] There was, however, one way to be original— he could work like the bees which "steal from this flower and that, but afterwards turn their pilferings into honey, which is their own; it is thyme and marjoram no longer."[3]

If he could never be sure of fully knowing anything in the world around him, at least within himself he had the fertile field of the senses and emotions which he could explore and come to understand through experience.

> I would rather understand myself well by self-study than by reading Cicero. In the experience that I have of myself I find enough to make me wise, if I were a good scholar. . . . I, who pretend to nothing else [than

---

*See my *The Spiritual Quest of Albert Camus* (Tuscaloosa AL: Portals Press, 1976) 12.

[2]*Montaigne. Selections from his writing, with an introductory essay by André Gide*, selections from John Florio's trans. (1603), intro. essay trans. Dorothy Bussy (repr. New York: McGraw-Hill, 1964; orig. *The Living Thoughts of Montaigne*, New York: Longmans, Green, 1939) 1.

[3]Montaigne, *Essays*, 56.

self-knowledge], find in myself such an infinite depth and variety that the sole fruit of my study is to make me feel how much I still have to learn. . . . It is from experience of myself that I attack human ignorance.[4]

Shortly before his death, Montaigne's father asked his son to translate into French for him a work of natural theology written during the fifteenth century by a Spanish physician, Raimond Sebond. This work set out to expound the Christian Faith in the light of "human and natural reason." Montaigne published his translation the year after his father died. Somewhat later he was to write his "In Defense of Raimond Sebond," by far the longest of his essays, and regarding which it has been aptly said that "Montaigne supports Sebond somewhat as the rope supports the hanged man, for his skepticism regarding the powers of human reason seems equally effectively to destroy the value of Sebond's arguments and those of his critics."[5] It should not be imagined, however, that this essay has much at all to do with Sebond or his writings which are clearly treated by Montaigne as a springboard, as opportunity to launch into an uninhibited discussion of his own thoughts regarding God and His relationship with creation. As one reads, one soon forgets that Sebond has anything to do with the matter being treated.

At the outset, Montaigne pays tribute to the work that supposedly is the subject of his essay:

> Its purpose is brave and courageous, for it undertakes, by human and natural reason, to establish and defend against the atheists all the articles of the Christian religion. To tell the truth, I find this work so solid and so successful that I do not think it possible to improve on that argument and believe that none other has equalled it.[6]

Of course, what Montaigne does not say at this point is whether he feels "that argument" and the realm in which it operates are valid; it is quite clear later that he thinks they are not. Yet, of its kind, and in its realm, he is undoubtedly speaking honestly when he says he knows no better—va-

---

[4]Ibid., 354-57.

[5]Montaigne, *In Defense of Raymond Sebond*, trans. Arthur Beattie (New York: Ungar Pub. Co., 1959) ix.

[6]Montaigne, *Apologie de Raymond Sebond* (Paris: Éditions Gallimard, 1962) 26 (A.T.).

lidity, however, is another matter. Montaigne's very next words are:

> As this work seemed to me to be too rich and too beautiful for an author
> whose name was so little known and of whom all we know is that he was
> Spanish and practised medicine at Toulouse about two hundred years ago,
> I enquired of Adrien Tournebu, who knows everything, what this book
> might be; he replied he thought it was some sort of refined extract from
> Thomas Aquinas's writings, for truly, only that mind, full as it was of an
> infinite learning and of an admirable subtlety, was capable of such imag-
> inations.[7]

On the surface it appears Montaigne is praising both Sebond and Aquinas;
but later--when he affirms that no human attributes have any power to give
man any understanding of God, and that all man's senses, through which
he receives all his knowledge, are hopelessly untrustworthy—it is clear that
he is damning them both, if obliquely.

Montaigne does not meet issues head-on; his method is more subtle:

> On many occasions (and I quite willingly engage in this) having under-
> taken as an exercise and a diversion to support an opinion contrary to my
> own, my mind, applying itself and turning in that direction, attaches me
> so completely to it that I can no longer find justification for my earlier
> position—and I abandon it. I tend to be carried away in whatever direc-
> tion I chance to lean, and then give myself totally to it.[8]

But as the sailing ship leans first to one side and then to the other as it tacks,
yet always returns to an upright position when at rest, so Montaigne has a
norm: skepticism about everything.

After praising Sebond and Aquinas, Montaigne first extols the values
of the human intellect:

> It is faith alone that keenly and with certainty embraces the lofty mys-
> teries of our religion. But that does not mean that it is not a very fine and
> praiseworthy enterprise to utilize in the service of our faith the natural
> and human tools that God has given us.[9]

But then, surprisingly, he launches an attack on the effects of Chris-

---

[7]Ibid., 27 (A.T.).

[8]Ibid., 294 (A.T.).

[9]Ibid., 28 (A.T.).

tianity: "Our religion is meant to remove vices; it covers them, feeds and incites them.[10] Furthermore, religion is as much a chance of birth as is nationality: "We receive our religion in our own way and by our own means, not in any way different from the way other religions are received. . . . We are Christians in the same manner that we are inhabitants of Perigord or Germans."[11] Montaigne's reader is now ready for an initial assault upon the human intellect:

> What does truth preach to us, when she tells us to flee from worldly philosophy, when she instills into us so often that our wisdom is nothing but foolishness before God; that, of all vanities, the most vain is man; that man who places such store by his knowledge, does not yet know what knowledge is, and that man who is nothing if he believes himself to be something only seduces and deludes himself.[12]

Having touched gently on the matter of human reason and its limitations (and in this last quotation he cites the apostle Paul), Montaigne switches to another tack, wondering if animals also participate in a religious experience.

> We can also say that elephants participate in measure in religion, inasmuch as after several washings and purifications one can see them raising their trunks like arms and fixing their eyes on the rising sun, remaining for a long time in meditation and contemplation at certain hours of the day of their own free will without any teaching or laws.[13]

Back he swings with a more telling attack on the intellect:

> Whatever participation we may have in the knowledge of the truth, it is not by our strength that we have acquired it. God has sufficiently taught us this by the witnesses he has chosen, from amongst the common, simple and ignorant people, to instruct us in his admirable secrets: our faith is not an acquisition we have made but a pure gift from the liberality of another. It is not by talk or by our understanding that we have received our religion, it is by authority and a command from outside ourselves.

[10]Ibid., 35 (A.T.).

[11]Ibid., 37 (A.T.).

[12]Ibid., 45 (A.T.).

[13]Ibid., 84 (A.T.).

The weakness of our judgment helps us more in it than does strength, and our blindness more than our clarity of perception. It is rather through our ignorance than our knowledge that we become participants in this divine learning. It is not surprising if our natural and earthly faculties cannot conceive of this supernatural and celestial knowledge. Let us approach it solely with obedience and subjection.[14]

What price now Sebond and Aquinas?

Away he tacks again—this time on an abstract consideration of the nature of God:

Of all the human and ancient opinions concerning religion, the one which seems to me the most likely and most defensible is that which recognizes God as an incomprehensible force, the originator and conserver of everything, totally good, perfect in all his ways, receiving and accepting the honor and reverence that humans render to him in whatever form, under whatever name and in whatever manner it may be.[15]

This suggests of course a form of Universalism that disregards the exclusive claims of Jesus Christ.

Then back he comes, and this time it appears he has found the hub and focus of the matter— Revelation:

Whatever anyone may preach to us, whatever we may learn, we must always remember that it is man who gives and man who receives; it is a mortal hand which presents it to us, and a mortal hand which accepts it. Only the things which come to us from heaven have the right and authority to persuade us; they alone have the marks of truth; and this we do not see with our own eyes or receive by our own powers: this holy and great image could not abide in such a wretched domicile if God did not prepare it for this purpose, reshape it, and fortify it by his special and supernatural grace and favor.[16]

Then, at once, almost without drawing a breath, Montaigne swings into a violent assault upon our senses through which, he says, all our knowledge comes to us, but which are totally unreliable because they are constantly vacillating and shifting according to our state of health, our emotions, cir-

---

[14]Ibid., 152 (A.T.).

[15]Ibid., 180 (A.T.).

[16]Ibid., 288 (A.T.).

cumstances, and every other condition of life: "The uncertainty of our senses renders uncertain everything they produce."[17] He goes as far as to suggest that we possibly lack one or more senses which, if we had them, would enable us to comprehend the meaning of life, and, without which, we are in a state of hopeless, unrelieved ignorance.

Having demonstrated forcefully that reason is impotent to advance in the knowledge of God, and that revelation cannot operate successfully because of the total unreliability of the senses through which it is received, he ends with what appears to be an affirmation of faith.

> Nor can man rise above himself and humanity, for he can only see with his eyes and seize with his hands. He will raise himself up if God lends him his hand in an extraordinary fashion; he will raise himself up, abandoning and renouncing his own strength and allowing himself to be raised and lifted up by strength which is purely divine. It is up to our Christian faith, and not Stoical virtue, to aspire to that divine and miraculous metamorphosis.[18]

It is this last quotation, and others like it sprinkled throughout Montaigne's work, that Gide calls "lightning-conductors, or better still, labels of lemonade or ginger-ale affixed upon bottles of whiskey when a regime has gone dry."[19] "Every time Montaigne speaks of Christianity" Gide continues, "it is with the strangest (sometimes one might almost say with the most malicious) impertinence. He often treats of religion, never of Christ. Not once does he refer to His words; one might almost doubt whether he had ever read the Gospels—or rather, one cannot doubt that he never read them seriously."[20] "He may have appeared a very good Catholic," Sainte-Beuve says of Montaigne, "except for not having been a Christian."[21]

But if Gide and Sainte-Beuve treat Montaigne's religious pretensions with disdain, T. S. Eliot is suspicious and even fearful of him.

---

[17]Ibid., 365 (A.T.).

[18]Ibid., 373 (A.T.).

[19]Gide, *Montaigne*, 18.

[20]Ibid., 16.

[21]Ibid., 18.

Now the great adversary against whom Pascal set himself, from the time
of his first conversations with M. de Saci at Port-Royal, was Montaigne.
One cannot destroy Pascal, certainly; but of all authors Montaigne is one
of the least destructible. You could as well dissipate a fog by flinging
hand-grenades into it. For Montaigne is a fog, a gas, a fluid, insidious
element. He does not reason, he insinuates, charms, and influences; or
if he reasons, you must be prepared for his having some other design upon
you than to convince you by his argument. . . . Indeed, by the time a
man knew Montaigne well enough to attack him, he would already be
thoroughly infected by him. . . . The picture of Montaigne which offers
itself first to our eyes, that of the original and independent solitary "per-
sonality," absorbed in amused analysis of himself, is deceptive. Montaigne's is no limited Pyrrhonism, like that of Voltaire, Renan, or
[Anatole] France. He exists, so to speak, on a plane of numerous con-
centric circles, the most apparent of which is the small inmost circle, a
personal puckish skepticism which can be easily aped if not imitated. But
what makes Montaigne a very great figure is that he succeeded. God
knows how—for Montaigne very likely did not know that he had done
it— it is not the sort of thing that men can observe about themselves, for
it is essentially bigger than the individual's consciousness—he succeeded in giving expression to the skepticism of *every* human being. For
every man who thinks and lives by thought must have his own skepticism, that which stops at the question, that which ends in denial, or that
which leads to faith and which is somehow integrated into the faith which
transcends it. [22]

Then, what of the *mind* of Montaigne? Man is a spiritual being and has
not only a soul but also "the spirit of the man which is in him" (1 Cor
2:11). It is this "spirit of the man" which enables him, if he uses it, to
"know the things of a man," "for who among men knoweth the things of
a man, save the spirit of the man which is in him?" "Now the natural [*psuchikos*, "soulical," governed by the emotions of the soul] man receives
not the things of the Spirit of God: for they are foolishness unto him; and
he cannot know them, because they are spiritually judged." (1 Cor 2:14)
The soulical man has a spirit but does not use it; he is carried away and
dominated by his soul, its emotions and desires. But the spiritual man uses
his spirit to communicate with the Spirit of God: "The things of God none

---

[22]T. S. Eliot, in Blaise Pascal, *Pensées*, trans. W. F. Trotter, intro. by Eliot (New
York: E. P. Dutton and Co., 1932) xiii.

knoweth, save the Spirit of God. But we received, not the spirit of the world, but the spirit which is of God; that we might know the things that are freely given to us by God.'' (1 Cor 2:11-12)

Now Montaigne is certainly not the soulical, animal, type, ever prey to the emotions and lusts of his soul; nor is he the spiritual person who, through his spirit, receives the Spirit of God in his quest to know the things of God. But he knows how to escape his soul's domination by living in his spirit (the spirit of the man which is in him). He proceeds out to the farthest limits of this spirit of the man in him, so as to be as free as possible from the disruptive, confusing stirrings of his soul, and then politely but firmly turns his back on God and His Spirit, and, from this vantage point, becomes an inquisitive spectator of the inner workings of the human soul.

But he does not approach this enquiry with logical, scientific method. The huntsman disciplines the foxhounds not to run off at a tangent, following the trail of rabbits which cross their path. Montaigne does precisely the opposite—he positively welcomes every rabbit, so that, ere long, it seems the fox is lost from view. When the hunt is over, nothing in particular has been accomplished, no fox caught, but the reader who has been led on this chase—unless he is very solidly grounded—is left with an impression, the suggestion of an attitude, he did not have before. He finds himself invited to doubt everything, and especially the things he formerly accepted without question. More seriously, he finds himself wondering if he should, if it is right to open up and consider the merits of the suggestions presented to him, and particularly their implications. He senses that, although he may not be sure what it is, something beyond mere fear or intrepid brashness should govern his response. Success to Montaigne is to bring his reader to this crisis; for Montaigne's mind is not just that of a passive skeptic, it reaches out to manipulate and subvert the minds of his readers, luring them towards his own attitude and outlook. He seeks to convey more an attitude than precise thoughts.

Inevitably one attributes a face, or at least an expression, to a writer one has read and thus come to know. A well-known statue of Voltaire wears a broad, sly grin—is it malicious, or does it just appear so on account of the almost skeletal thinness of the one who wears it? With Montaigne it would more likely be a smile, but inscrutable and aloof, and probably only just discernible, perhaps not unlike that of the Mona Lisa, but with a vestige of an additional element—the indirect glance of the quizzical scheming conniver. But this is mere conjecture. One thing is certain: Montaigne had a powerful influence on the thinkers who followed him, particularly Descartes and Pascal, and indeed on the subsequent history of thought in Western civilization.

CHAPTER 5

Descartes

———— // ————

"Descartes useless and questionable!" Pascal does not mince words.

> I cannot forgive Descartes. In all his philosophy he would quite willingly
> have done without God; but he could not avoid attributing to Him an ini-
> tial flick of the fingers which set the world in motion—beyond this, how-
> ever, he has no further use for God.[1]

We have here about one half of the words Pascal devotes to Descartes in
his *Pensées*. Had he known the extraordinary influence Descartes was to
have on Western thought, he doubtless would have written much more. Or
did he feel, as did T. S. Eliot, that in these few words he had "laid his
finger on the place of weakness"?[2]

Essentially, in his writings treating spiritual matters, Descartes de-
throned God the Spirit and deified in His place human reason. He offered
an alternative, an escape, which, in the succeeding centuries, many gladly
embraced. One of his most recent and devoted acolytes, Jean-Paul Sartre,
sought, in a multitude of words, to develop the basic concept of his mentor
into an elaborate substitute for the revelation of Christian faith.

---

[1]Blaise Pascal, *Oeuvres complètes. Texte établi et annoté par Jacques Chevalier*, Bibliothèque de la Pléiade 34 (Paris: Éditions Gallimard, 1954) 1137 (A.T.).

[2]Blaise Pascal, *Pensées*, trans. W. F. Trotter, foreword by T. S. Eliot, Everyman's
Library (New York: E. P. Dutton and Co., 1932) xviii.

Like Montaigne, Descartes also has a famous dictum, this one appetizing game for many a hungry scholar: "I think, therefore I am." (In Latin, "Cogito, ergo sum"; in French, "Je pense, donc je suis.") It is a simple phrase that, on the surface, appears innocuous enough, but which, on closer scrutiny, can be seen to reveal an attitude. After all, if my very existence is dependent upon or proven by my thinking, then the thinking is basic to everything that relates to me. It is but a short step thence to conclude that through thinking, reasoned thought, or intellectual activity, I can reach all the conclusions I need for a complete life; that a spiritual or metaphysical realm, beyond what reason can prove, has little if any significance or does not even exist; and that man is indeed sufficient, after the manner of W. E. Henley in his poem Invictus: "I am the master of my fate, I am the captain of my soul."—the alpha and omega of the philosophy of Sartre.

Many have sought to establish or demolish Descartes by seeking to validate or invalidate his dictum "I think, therefore I am." I cite only two, André Gide and Gilbert Ryle, who seem to me by their approach to display not only a grasp of the thought (and thought deals with knowledge), but also a certain wisdom in their handling of the matter (and wisdom is using one's knowledge effectively, focusing it helpfully). Gide avoids the trap of taking either the dictum or himself too seriously, and thus escapes becoming bogged down in an intellectual maze where Descartes might wish him to be; Gilbert Ryle is clear and understandable, even to one who makes no pretense of being a philosopher. First Gide:

> *"I think, therefore I am*—
>
> It is the *therefore* that I stumble over.
>
> *I think* and I am; there would be more truth in: I feel, therefore I am—or even: I believe therefore I am—for that is tantamount to saying:
>
> I think that I am.
>
> I believe that I am.
>
> I feel that I am.
>
> Now of the three propositions, the last appears to me the truest, the only true one; because, in the final analysis, I think that I am does not necessarily imply that I am. Nor does: I believe that I am. There is as much audacity in going from one to the other as to make "I believe that God is," a proof of the existence of God. Whereas: "I feel that I am. . . .—here I am both judge and participant. How could I be in error in this proposition?
>
> *I think therefore that I am*—I think *that I am* therefore I am. Because I cannot think except it be about something.—

Example: I think that God is . . . or . . . I think that the angles of a triangle are equal to two right angles, *therefore I am*—Then it is the I which is impossible to establish; . . . therefore that is—I remain in the neuter.

I think: therefore I am.

One might just as well say: I suffer, I breathe, I feel: therefore I am. Because if one cannot think without being, one can certainly be without thinking.

But as long as I stay with feeling, I am not involved with thinking that I am. By this act of thinking I am made conscious of my being, but at the same time I cease from simply being: I am a thinking being.

I think therefore I am is the same as saying: I think that I am, and this *therefore* which seems to be the balance beam of the scales has no significance. There is nothing in the two trays of the scale that I have not put in them, that is to say the same thing. $X = X$. It is in vain that I juggle the terms, nothing comes out of it except, after a certain time, a splitting headache and the desire to go out into the fresh air to walk it off."[3]

Some would question Gide saying, "If one cannot think without being, one can certainly be without thinking." Following my own counsel of not taking all this too seriously, while, I hope, not being overly facetious, I cannot resist a little anecdote. There was a country village in England with the village pub on one side of the green. The old man of the community could be found daily, and most of the day, on a bench in front of this pub. A visitor asked him, "And now, my good man, what do you do with yourself all day?" The reply was simple and concise: "Sometimes I sits and thinks, and sometimes I just sits." This is a healthy antidote to the complex, dry, and rather smug cerebrality of Descartes.

Gilbert Ryle approaches the subject as a philosopher. He coins a phrase—"category mistake"—for what he demonstrates to be the fundamental error of Descartes's theory.

When two terms belong to the same category, it is proper to construct conjunctive propositions embodying them. Thus a purchaser may say that he bought a left-hand glove and a right-hand glove, but not that he bought a left-hand glove and a right-hand glove, and a pair of gloves. "She came home in a flood of tears and a sedan-chair" is a well-known joke based

[3]André Gide, *Romans, récits et soties, oeuvres lyriques,* intro. Maurice Nadeau, Bibliothèque de la Pléiade 135 (Paris: Éditions Gallimard, 1958) 271 (A.T.).

on the absurdity of conjoining terms of different types. It would have been equally ridiculous to construct the disjunction "She came either in a flood of tears or else in a sedan-chair." Now the dogma of the Ghost in the Machine does just this. It maintains that there exist both bodies and minds; that there occur physical processes and mental processes; that there are mechanical causes of corporeal movements and mental causes of corporeal movements. I shall argue that these and other analogous conjunctions are absurd; but, it must be noticed, the argument will not show that either of the illegitimately conjoined propositions is absurd in itself. I am not, for example, denying that there occur mental processes. Doing long division is a mental process and so is making a joke. But I am saying that the phrase "there occur mental processes" does not mean the same sort of thing as "there occur physical processes," and, therefore, that it makes no sense to conjoin or disjoin the two.[4]

Now the two concepts of "thinking" and "being" in Descartes's dictum are in quite separate and different categories, and there is no logical justification for linking them with "therefore." It is interesting to note that Gilbert Ryle explains in philosophic terms what Gide explained in literary when he said that "I feel that I am" is preferable to "I believe that I am" or "I think that I am," because in that phrase the one who is speaking is both judge and participant; there is a relationship, a common ground between the terms: at least to a degree, they are in the same category.

But my thesis is that Descartes's error of "category mistake" far transcends propositions he devised; it is found in his very mode of thinking in that he claims a form of revelation in a realm where he shouldn't—the world of dreams— and then uses his reason to seek to establish spiritual verities. Had he considered Montaigne more carefully ("It is rather through our ignorance than our knowledge that we become participants in this divine learning. It is not surprising if our natural and earthly faculties cannot conceive of this supernatural and celestial knowledge."*) he might have been more cautious before seeking to establish the infinite by his finite mind, or the eternal, being ephemeral himself. But first a brief outline of his life.

---

[4]René Descartes, *Collection of critical Essays,* ed. Willis Doney (New York: Doubleday and Co. Inc., 1967) 350.

*See above, p. 48.

Descartes was born 31 March 1596 at La Haye, a little town in Touraine, about 150 miles southwest of Paris. His family, while not aristocratic, claimed to be of the gentry: his father was a councillor in the Bretagne parliament. Descartes's mother died one year after his birth, leaving a sickly child with "a dry cough and a pale complexion." Everyone thought he would die young.

At the age of ten he entered the Jesuit college of La Flèche where he proved himself an excellent student even if frail in health. He early showed a penchant for mathematics which he liked because of the certainty of its reasoning. On leaving college he completed his education by studying dancing, horseback riding, and fencing in which latter he became quite an expert. In 1616 he took his baccalaureate exams and his law degree before the faculty of Paris, just a few days apart. Two years later, at age twenty-two, he went to Holland where he enlisted in the army under Maurice of Nassau, the Prince of Orange. The following year he went first to Denmark and then to Germany where he joined the army of the Duke of Bavière. In Germany, during the winter of 1619, there occurred the decisive event of his life.

During a night of ecstasy and passion, during the course of three successive dreams, he came to a certainty regarding his vocation and was dazzled by a remarkable revelation. The heart of this revelation is, without doubt, the intuitive sense of a fundamental harmony between the laws of nature and the laws of mathematics, a sense of intuition which was to lead him, by way of progression and consequence, on the one hand to seek new and sure principles for a philosophy of nature and for a philosophy of the mind, and on the other, to take up again, to state precisely, to realize the Pythagorean hope of subordinating the universe to numbers, and, at the same time, to discover a way by which man, by his dexterity, could have a sure grasp of things.[5]

It appears that Descartes renounced military life in 1620 and, after extensive travels in Germany and Holland, returned to France in 1622. Some six years later, for the sake of his health and because it was a wealthy and orderly country, he moved to Holland where he stayed for more than twenty years, living the life of a gentleman. From this point on he took little in-

[5]René Descartes, *Oeuvres et Lettres*, Bibliothèque de la Pléiade 40 (Paris: Éditions Gallimard, 1953) 10 (A.T.).

58 REASON AND REVELATION

terest in what anyone else wrote or had written, so certain was he that he himself was on the road to truth. In 1635 a certain Hélène, probably a servant woman, bore him a daughter; when his little Francine later died at the age of five, he suffered deeply.

He prepared for publication a little work on metaphysics entitled *Le Monde* (*Treatise on the World and on Light*), but, when Galileo was condemned for his ideas regarding the rotation of the earth, he suppressed the work, and indeed decided never to publish anything, lest he upset the tranquillity of his life-style or cause friction between himself and the church. However, in 1637 he decided to test public opinion and published three little treatises (*Geometry, Dioptric,* and *Meteors*), and prefaced the three with the famous *Discours de la méthode* (*Discourse on the Method*).

Discours de la méthode indeed established Descartes's fame, his ideas on physics being well received by the general public. But certain church officials accused him of atheism and Pelagianism. He disliked any opposition and, becoming excessively diplomatic, did all he could to work his way back into the good graces of all concerned. In 1649 Queen Christina of Sweden invited him to her court to instruct her in his philosophy. After some misgivings, he went. A few months later, in February 1650, he caught cold which quickly developed into pneumonia, and nine days later died.

Now for the two "category mistakes" in Descartes's mode of thinking—first the dreamworld revelation, and then reason trespassing in spiritual things. The first occurred in November 1619 when Descartes was in Germany

> where wars which still have not finished had called me; and, while I was returning to the army after attending the crowning of the emperor, the onset of winter caught me in a place where, finding no conversation which interested me, and, fortunately, having no cares or passions which troubled me, I remained all day alone shut up in a warm room, where, at my leisure, I could give myself to my thoughts.[6]

One night he experienced a dream that came to him in three episodes. He

> dreams first that a boisterous wind swirls around him in the street, whilst he walks with difficulty, leaning to his left, and trying to reach the church of the college (of la Flèche), in order to pray there. At the moment when he turns around to be polite to a man he had neglected to greet, the wind

Ibid., 132 (A.T.).

pushes him back violently against the church. Soon a person, in the middle of the college courtyard, tells him that someone he knows has something to give him—a melon. He experiences pain on waking up, turns over on his right side, and prays to God to be preserved from the evil effect of his dream. Later, having fallen back to sleep again, he has a further dream which terrifies him, he is woken up by a loud noise as of thunder, and notices a lot of fiery sparks in his room. Finally, in the third dream, he sees a dictionary on his table and a *Corpus poetarum* [book of poetry], open at a passage by Ausone: *quod vitae sectabor iter?* (What path in life shall I follow?). An unknown man presents him a piece of poetry, the words *Est et Non* catch his eye.[7]

Now, Descartes's own interpretation:

In the first dream, the melon offered to Descartes symbolizes "the charms of solitude, but presented by purely human solicitations." The wind which drives the staggering pedestrian towards the church is none other than an evil spirit which tries "to cast him by force into a place where his purpose was to go voluntarily. That is why God did not allow him to be carried away, even to a holy place, by a Spirit which he had not sent."
The thunder clap of the second dream is "the signal of the Spirit of Truth which was descending on Descartes in order to possess him."
In the last dream, the dictionary represents "all the sciences gathered together," and the collection of poems, Philosophy joined to Wisdom. For M. Descartes "did not believe that one should be so surprised to discover that the poets, even the ones who make light of things, were full of sayings which were more weighty, more sensible and better expressed than what one finds in the writings of Philosophers. He attributed this marvel to the divineness of the Ecstasy and the strength of the Imagination, which brings out the seeds of wisdom (which are in the minds of all men even as sparks of fire are in stones) with much more ease and much more brilliance than can the Philosophers' Reason." "What path of life shall I follow?" is the question posed by moral theology. The "Yes or No" [Est et Non], borrowed from Pythagoras, corresponds to the truth and falsehood in secular learning.[8]

Freud showed interest in only the first dream in which he saw guilt and,

---

[7]Jacques Maritain, *Le songe de Descartes* (Paris: Buchet/Chastel, 1944) 4 (A.T.).

[8]Pierre Frédérix, *M. René Descartes* (Paris: Éditions Gallimard, 1959) 50.

predictably, frustration of sexual desire.[9] Baillet assures us that Descartes was sober that night, and, indeed, that he had drunk no alcohol during the preceding three months.[10] It has been suggested that Descartes trafficked in occultism or was influenced by Rosicrucian illuminism or medieval mysticism. Whether there is any truth in any of this (none of which represents a very propitious beginning for one who supposedly later totally freed human thought), one thing seems clear: this three-episode dream, which seemed so significant to Descartes, was apparently neither spiritual nor from God. We shall later deal with Pascal's experience of revelation, and find it to be of an altogether different order.

Although Descartes's *Discourse on the Method* was not published until 1637, it was conceived in 1619, in Germany, during the time Descartes had the dreams referred to above. The dictum ''I think, therefore I am'' almost certainly dates from the same time, as does the following rational proof of the existence of God, to which I have earlier alluded as reason trespassing in spiritual things.

> Reflecting on the fact that I doubted, and that, as a consequence, my being was not completely perfect, for I saw clearly that knowing was a greater perfection than doubting, I was minded to find out from where I had learned to think about something which was more perfect than myself; and I recognized clearly that it must be from some nature which was, in fact, more perfect than mine. Concerning thoughts which I had about several other things such as the sky, the earth, light, heat and a thousand other things, I wasn't so troubled to discover where they came from, since, not observing anything in them which appeared to make them superior to me, I could believe that, if they really existed, they were dependent upon my nature since it possessed a measure of perfection; and if they did not exist, that I was creating them out of nothing, that is to say that their presence in me was the fruit of my defectiveness. But the same could not be said concerning the idea of a being who was more perfect than mine; for to create this out of nothingness was manifestly impossible; and as it is no less repugnant to good sense to regard what is more perfect as being a consequence of and dependent upon what is less perfect, than it is to imagine something coming out of nothing, I could not regard the

[9]Ibid., 51.

[10]*Descartes par Lui-même*, (par) Samuel S. de Sacy (Paris) Éditions de Seuil (1956) (Ecrivains de toujours 36) 67.

idea of perfection as coming out of myself. So that the only reasonable conclusion was that it had been put in me by a nature which was truly more perfect than I, and which, furthermore, possessed in itself all the perfection I could imagine, to put it in a nutshell—God.[11]

The danger in all of this is that the reader may be drawn into thinking in this manner, into this frame of thought, which is sterile and powerless to convince the normal, healthily complete (body, soul, and spirit) person of the existence of God. In fact, it not only is unconvincing but often produces distaste, and sometimes even repugnance. I found myself one day in an intellectual group which included a physicist who was a great admirer of Descartes. This physicist proceeded through the reasoning outlined above to triumphantly demonstrate (so he thought) the existence of God. When he had finished, I broke in with, "I think I just heard a sigh of relief in heaven. God relieved to be permitted to exist by kind permission of the reasoning of Descartes."—a deliberate introduction of another dimension, and change in the frame of thought.

Like Montaigne, Descartes never mentions Jesus Christ, who brought God near. If he doesn't turn his back on God, as did Montaigne (see above, p. 51), he views Him from afar, regarding himself as a "thing which thinks"[12] and God as having an essence and as also existing because "from the mere fact that I cannot conceive of God except as existing, it follows that existence is inseparable from Him and therefore that He does, actually in fact, exist."[13]

At the Battle of Copenhagen, a subordinate drew then Vice-Admiral Nelson's attention to a signal flying at the yardarm of his commander-in-chief's flagship, which signal ordered him to withdraw. Nelson raised his telescope to his blind eye, said he saw nothing, and proceeded on his course. Descartes did not have a blind eye; but he took the telescope and reversed it, magnifying himself, his intellect and reasoning powers, and minifying God, reducing Him to some*thing* small and far away which could be contained and categorized by the human mind.

---

[11]Descartes, *Oeuvres et Lettres,* 148 (A.T.).

[12]Ibid., 277 (A.T.).

[13]Ibid., 313 (A.T.).

CHAPTER 6

Pascal

————— // —————

Blaise Pascal was born during June 1623 into a family whose origins were from the lesser nobility and the upper bourgeoisie. His birthplace, Clermont-Ferrand, was the capital of Auvergne, about 280 miles due south of Paris. Most of his life was spent in the vicinity of his birthplace or at Paris.

He had one sister Gilberte, three years older than himself, and another, Jacqueline, two years younger. His mother died shortly after the birth of Jacqueline, her place in the family soon to be taken by Gilberte who later married, becoming Mme Périer. From his earliest years Blaise showed extraordinary genius. At sixteen he wrote a treatise on conic sections which heralded modern projective geometry. At nineteen he invented, constructed, and offered for sale the first calculating machine. Later he gave Pascal's law to physics, proved the existence of the vacuum, and helped to establish the science of hydrodynamics. He created the mathematical theory of probability, and made important speculations in the early development of infinitesimal calculus. Despite these extraordinary attainments in the realm of science, it is rather for his contributions to thought on philosophical and spiritual matters, most of which came after his spiritual conversion at the age of thirty-one, that he has become universally famous. He died at the early age of thirty-nine.

The Pascal family's religion was typical of their station in life of that day. The children recited the catechism, read the Bible, church history, and even the church fathers. They took their religion seriously, but it evidently was no more than one aspect of the family life rather than a governing influence over the whole. The father Etienne, rather like Descartes, made a convenient distinction between religion and the authority of the Church of Rome on the one hand, and science and reason on the other. This equilibrium, however, was to be rudely disrupted by what appeared to be a chance incident which, coming upon the family during the winter of 1646, late in Blaise's twenty-second year, marked the starting point of a totally new spiritual orientation for every member.

It was a bitter, icy, January day when a messenger came running to the house of Etienne Pascal to inform him that two gentlemen were about to meet to settle a point of honor by duelling in a field outside Rouen where the Pascal family was living at the time. Knowing that Cardinal Richelieu was intent on stamping out the practice of duelling, Etienne decided to go at once to the site to seek to dissuade the participants. When informed that his horses were inadequately shod to venture forth on the icy roads, he decided to go alone, and on foot. He had not gone far, however, when he slipped on the ice and fell, seriously injuring his hip.

Once back in his home he did not call a physician but sent for two gentlemen who had a reputation in the neighbourhood as bonesetters. He was unaware that he was inviting into his house two devoted young Christians who had recently been converted by a Jansenist priest. These two young men spent three months in the Pascal household, bringing with them an altogether new approach to Christianity. They spoke with zeal and fervor, and the sacrificial attitude of their life corroborated their words. They brought with them books on Jansenism which they placed in the hands of Blaise who was very soon captivated by the precision, Calvinistic thoroughness, and detail of Jansenist teaching.

Once convinced himself, Blaise set about seeking to convert his sister Jacqueline and his father to his newfound faith. Before the year was out, the whole family, including the eldest daughter Gilberte and her husband, had been won over. From the outset, however, there was a distinction between Blaise and his younger sister Jacqueline—he was quick and extreme, and clearly his brilliant intellect had been enthralled by the almost mathematical, systematic perfection of the Jansenist teaching; the more stable Jacqueline was more careful before committing herself. Once convinced, however, Jacqueline set her face resolutely to go the whole way, and she never looked back. Unhappily, with Blaise it was a different story.

Was it that he had been influenced by his father's attitude of a departmentalized mind which could shut off or switch on the realm of religious occupation at will? Whatever the cause, his first experience, or "conversion," was not lasting in its effect. Perhaps it was this incompleteness and inadequacy in his experience which prompted him later to write in his *Pensées,* "Men often take their imagination for their hearts; and they think they are converted as soon as they think of being converted."[1]

Pascal scholars call this his "intellectual conversion." His experience of the heart, which was to effect a transformation of his whole attitude and outlook, followed some eight years later in 1654. Jacqueline, on the other hand, as already mentioned, was total in her commitment from the outset and, during the ensuing years, became a kind of conscience to her brother which, through all his errings, repeatedly beckoned him back to the full way. In this she played much the same role in her brother's life, though for a considerably longer period, as Stephen in the life of Paul (see above, p. 3)—but more of this in due course.

What was it that produced this critical yet incomplete effect upon the life of Blaise Pascal? Without doubt there was something infectious about the demeanor of the two missionary-minded bonesetters. The precision and austerity of the Jansensist doctrine, as already mentioned, must have appealed to his mathematical mind, and there may have been additional factors which conspired to produce in Blaise the conviction that he numbered among the elect—yet there was something lacking which left his spiritual life unfulfilled.

It can be generally stated that today we have a counterpart to the Jansenist in the Fundamentalist, and to the Jesuit in the Liberal. From today's revivals and evangelistic campaigns comes many a soul who has been convinced and may also have made a "decision," but who nevertheless knows there is still something he lacks. Some years ago the author talked with a young man who testified that on four different occasions he had signed "decision cards," and had subsequently made two other "decisions," then one day something dawned upon him and he *knew.* Paul says, "when it was the good pleasure of God . . . to reveal His Son in me . . . " (Gal 1:15)—this represents something of an entirely different order from a "decision." Although it can be assumed that a desire to receive on the part of the seeker is a prerequisite to his finding, yet the "when" of the matter is

---

[1]Blaise Pascal, *Pensées* (Paris: Garnier Frères, 1964) 164 (A.T.).

governed "by the good pleasure of God" who alone knows the true motive, the measure of the desire, and the consequent state of readiness of the soul. Thus God calls through Jeremiah and says, "And ye shall seek me, and find me, when ye shall search for me with all your heart." (Jer 29:13). Seemingly Jacqueline's conversion was wholehearted from the beginning whereas her brother took the next eight years to arrive at that position.

This new spiritual movement entered the Pascal family through the Jansenists, and Jansenism and Port Royal (the convent in Paris that was the home of Jansenism) were to be the context of the spiritual development of Blaise and Jacqueline. This then is a good point to pause and examine briefly the origins of Jansenism and the Jansenist-Jesuit controversy that later, after his real conversion, was so much to preoccupy Blaise.

Every movement of true spiritual renewal has at its heart fresh revelation of the mercy and grace of God; Jansenism was no exception. Early in the seventeenth Century, Cornelius Jansen, then Bishop of Ypres, felt inadequacy in his spiritual life and set himself to seek the remedy. As he studied, particularly the works of Augustine, spiritual illumination dawned upon him, and what he saw he sought to lay out in systematic form in a lengthy writing that came to be known as the "Augustinus." The emphasis of this work was that everything in salvation is attributable to grace, nothing to the works of man, and very little to his freedom of will to choose. This doctrine at once evoked enthusiasm on the part of some; others, however, particularly the Jesuits, were incensed and accused the Jansenists of being so ruthless in their teaching as to discard men and women, sacrificing them to what they perceived as truth. Jansenists were raising barriers everywhere, the Jesuits said, and setting themselves up as the sole proprietors and expositors of the true way. The Jansenists were so cruelly harsh, Jesuits charged, that in their insistence on truth they were becoming inhuman.

From their side the Jansenists accused the Jesuits of being more concerned with men's interests and passions, which they defended by their casuistry, than with the truth. The Jansenists said that Jesuits adjusted and diluted the truth to make it attractive to every man, and, moreover, that they were more concerned to maintain their wide influence over the many, by compromise if necessary, than to proclaim the truth as it was in reality with the challenge it provoked. The Jesuits, said the Jansenists, were too human and not spiritual enough.

Thus began one of the many theological disputes of history in which each side resorted to reason to defend its position. In spiritual things, once the attitude is defensive and the weapon is reason, it seems a foregone conclusion that only loss can come from the ensuing conflict; this was certainly the case in the Jansenist-Jesuit controversy. Reason is competent in the realm over which it has jurisdiction—natural created things—but it cannot correlate and set in proper order the verities of the spiritual realm which is above and incomprehensible to it.

There has perhaps been no other doctrinal point in the whole history of the church that has produced more controversy than the dispute as to whether man has freedom of will to choose his destiny or whether all, even the inclining of the heart of man God-ward, which causes him to choose in that direction, is attributable to grace. The seeming chasm between these two "minds" is minimized if not eliminated when one recognizes that God's foreknowledge (which is eternal, outside time) preceded his predestining (Rom 8:28). Evidently, in the suffering of his heart, God foresaw that some would refuse while others would receive him. These latter he predestined to be conformed to the image of his son, and gave all the grace needful to accomplish this. But what does he do concerning the rest? If He had foreseen that they would reject Him, it would only be logical and reasonable (notice these last two adjectives!) for Him to wash His hands of them and leave them to their self-chosen end. But He does not do this. The Scriptures add paradoxically that God "willeth* that all men should be saved, and come to the knowledge of the truth" (1 Tim 2:4). This accounts for the conduct of the Lord Jesus who, though it is affirmed that he "knew . . . who it was that should betray him" (John 6:64), nevertheless did all he could, right up to the last moment, to try to win Judas Iscariot. Here is a mystery our reason can never fathom. It is one aspect of the love of God.

Among fundamentalists there are those who grasp the tenets in their minds, and cleave to them with a sort of dogged legalism; there are others whose hearts have been touched, and through whom, as a consequence, the grace of God is felt. It appears that Pascal, at his first conversion, fell into the former category; Jacqueline, from the outset of her spiritual life, was of the latter. A sad incident is cited which occurred in 1647, just one year after Pascal's first conversion. A certain Franciscan friar, Jacques Forton, reputed to be a philosopher, came to Rouen and began to expound

---

*Greek *thelō,* to wish or to desire; not *boulomai,* a deliberate exercise of the will.

privately certain unorthodox views regarding the birth of Christ. Pascal charged him with heresy, and persuaded M. de Bellay, who was acting in the place of the archbishop in the latter's absence, to insist that Forton sign a recantation, which he did. But Pascal refused to let the matter rest there, and insisted, despite the admonishment of older and wiser heads, that Forton be punished by being brought before an ecclesiastical council.[2] Much zeal was apparent in this, perhaps even truth, but not much grace.

On the other side of the coin, the Jansenist center, the convent of Port Royal, which Jacqueline entered shortly after her father's death, was warm with evangelical fervor, and with grace. Mère Angélique, who had a position of considerable responsibility in the convent, wrote with much satisfaction, "Someone is always converted when M. Singlin preaches, our New Church is always full." History suggests that the deeper the movement is spiritually, the stronger will be the emphasis on grace.

Shortly after his father's accident and the stay of the two Jansenists in the home, Blaise became once again absorbed with science, and spiritual considerations began to slip into the background. Of the next eight years there is little to say that relates to our subject here—it was essentially a downhill story spiritually. Pascal's interest in science led into a taste for society and its luxuries; he indulged himself in fine clothes and carriages; he learned to play dice and cards. He formed friendships with some of the nobility, and began to adapt himself to their ways in his desire to be accepted. It is even surmised that he fell in love with Charlotte Gouffier, the sister of his best friend, the duke of Roannez. In the midst of all this it is recorded that Jacqueline asked for prayer that her brother be converted[3]— evidence of the value she placed on his first "conversion" in the light of subsequent developments.

Was it a sense of failure that brought Pascal back again to spiritual considerations? His calculating maching did not sell. His scientific friends, admiring though they were, had no idea of the far-reaching future significance of his mathematical work. Court society had received him with polite and curious wonder, but never with that wholehearted acclaim that ambition craves— he was forever an outsider in their world. If he had loved, and it had been Charlotte Gouffier, it was in vain because the exclusive

[2]Humfrey Jordan, *Blaise Pascal* (London: Williams and Norgate, 1909) 52.

[3]Morris Bishop, *Pascal. The Life of a Genius* (New York: Reynal and Hitchcock, 1936) 125.

rules of French high society were too strong for even his genius to break. He was later to write that

> those who are capable of inventing are rare; the greater number wish only to follow, and refuse glory to those inventors who seek it by their inventions; and if they persist in trying to obtain glory, and in scorning those who do not invent, the others give them peculiar names and would be glad to beat them. So let no one pride himself on his ingenuity, or let him keep his self-complacency to himself.[4]

In September 1654, Pascal visited Jacqueline in her convent. A few months later, in a letter to her sister, Jacqueline describes how she found her brother on this occasion.

> Towards the end of last September he came to me and opened his heart in a way which wrung mine, saying that in the midst of all his great occupations, and among all those things which might have combined to attach him to the world (things which we naturally thought he was thoroughly enjoying) he had been so longing to get away from all that, having so great an aversion for the follies and amusements of the world and being incessantly stung by his conscience, that he had now broken away from everything as never before; he had known nothing approaching it. And yet, for all that, he felt completely abandoned from God and with no attraction whatever of that sort. But he believed he was merely making an intellectual struggle to find God; it was not genuine movement of himself towards God. In his present detachment he felt that if only he could recover his former sentiments towards God he could overcome the horrible temptations which assailed him to resist God's grace.[5]

Blaise returned frequently to the convent in those days to talk with his sister. Apparently it was seeing in her the peace and assurance he lacked which both drew him and spurred him on in his God-ward quest, this time with his whole heart. It was not until after his death that there was discovered, sewn into the lining of his doublet, a folded parchment containing a scribbled sheet of paper on which he recorded the thoughts and emotions that came to him on the night of his genuine conversion—a night during which certainty dawned upon him spiritually, wholly apart from any ac-

---

[4]Pascal, *Pensées,* 154 (A.T.).

[5]Ernest Mortimer, *Blaise Pascal. The Life and Work of a Realist* (London: Methuen and Co., Ltd.; New York: Harper, 1959) 121.

tivity or reasoning of his mind. Here is what was written on that paper.*

The Year of Grace, 1654
Monday, 23rd November, Feast of S. Clement, Pope and Martyr,
and of others in the martyrology.
The Eve of Saint Chrysogonus, martyr, and others.
From about half past ten in the evening until about half past twelve.

 1 FIRE
 2 *God of Abraham, God of Isaac, God of Jacob,*
 3 *not of philosophers and scholars.*
 4 Certainty. Certainty. Feeling, Joy, Peace.
 5 God of Jesus Christ.
 6 *My God and Your God.*   (Jn 20:17)
 7 *Thy God will be my God.*   (Ruth 1:16)
 8 Forgetfulness of the world and of everything except God.
 9 He is to be found only in the ways taught in the Gospel.
10 Greatness of the human soul.
11 *O righteous Father, the world knew thee not, but I knew* (Jn 17:25)
    thee.
12 Joy, Joy, Joy, tears of joy.
13 I fell away from Him.
14 *They have forsaken me the fountain of living waters.*   (Jer 2:13)
15 My God, wilt Thou forsake me?
16 Let me never be separated from Him.
17 *And this is life eternal, thay they should know thee the only* (Jn 17:3)
    true God, and him whom thou didst send, Jesus Christ.
18 Jesus Christ.
19 Jesus Christ.
20 I fell away from Him. I fled from Him, renounced and cru-
    cified Him.
21 Let me never be separated from Him.
22 He is kept only by the ways taught in the Gospel.
23 Renunciation, total and sweet.
24 Total submission to Jesus Christ and to my director.

---

*Line numbers, italics to indicate quotations from the Bible, and source citations are mine.

25 Eternally in a state of joy for a day's trial on earth.
26 *I will not forget thy words.* Amen. (Ps 119:16)[6]

Lines 1-12 of the memorial could as well have been written by Paul at his conversion (see above, p. 9), by Augustine at his (see above, pp. 22-23), or by Aquinas at his (see above, pp. 24-25). All four received something by revelation that transcended the realm and powers of human reason, and conveyed certainty, joy, and peace. For all four (statedly so in the case of Paul, Augustine, and Pascal) the revelation was of Jesus Christ. But Pascal's lines 13-16 and 20-21 express an experience peculiar to him— fear, fear that he might fall away from God. During the two brief hours on the night of 23 November 1654, Pascal was first flooded by a *feeling* (French *sentiment*) of certainty and assurance, but then immediately assailed by a recurring sense of at least apprehension if not outright fear, which occupies must of the latter half of the memorial. I believe there is an explanation to this.

There are two sorts of second-conversion experience, those that are necessary because the first experience was based on an inadequate presentation of the Gospel, and those that also are necessary, but this time because the response on the first occasion was less than wholehearted to what was a full and adequate presentation. The former produces objective difficulties with regard to faith, as we shall shortly see, but the latter produces subjective difficulties. Pascal's problem was of the latter type.

> And it came to pass, that, while Apollos was at Corinth, Paul having passed through the upper country came to Ephesus, and found certain disciples: and he said unto them, Did ye receive the Holy Ghost when ye believed? And they said unto him, Nay, we did not so much as hear whether the Holy Ghost was. And he said, Into what then were ye baptized? And they said, Into John's baptism. And Paul said, John baptized with the baptism of repentance, saying unto the people, that they should believe on him which should come after him, that is, on Jesus. And when they heard this, they were baptized into the name of the Lord Jesus. And when Paul had laid his hands upon them, the Holy Ghost came on them; and they spake with tongues, and prophesied. And they were in all about twelve men. (Acts 19:1-7)

---

[6]Blaise Pascal, *Oeuvres complètes. Texte établi et annoté par Jacques Chevalier*, Bibliothèque de la Pléiade 34 (Paris: Éditions Gallimard, 1954) 553 (A.T.).

Apparently these twelve disciples were the fruit of the preaching of Apollos who was in Ephesus before Paul, and whom Priscilla and Aquila, when they heard him speak, took on one side and "expounded unto him the way of God more carefully" (Acts 18:26). The problem for these twelve would have appeared to be Apollos and Paul, and possibly God. First one preaches one thing to them, then along comes another who tells them that what they were taught is inadequate and incomplete. How can they be sure that a third, and maybe even a fourth, will not follow, each insisting that what he adds is essential? Whom could they trust, and why did God allow such a thing? Their problem was objective. This explains why the Holy Spirit did not come upon them after Paul had spoken. Paul had to go beyond his usual practice and lay his hands upon them, whereupon they spoke with tongues. And all of this was necessary because of an initial inadequate presentation that, in their innocence, restricted their experience.

In Pascal's case, the initial presentation of the two zealous, Jansenist bonesetters was apparently wholly adequate, as evidenced by its completely transforming effect upon his sister Jacqueline, when relayed to her through him. But (and strangely enough this is not uncommon) the one who relayed the message did not respond to it wholly himself. God will not prop up the less than wholly committed soul—if He did so it would only encourage halfheartedness and mediocrity. Thus, as no man has the power to hold himself to God, sooner or later, the partially committed will drift and fall away; and this is just what happened to Pascal. When he awoke to what had befallen him he became desperate, as noted in Jacqueline's letter (see above, p. 69). During the night he was truly converted he saw not only Jesus Christ but also, and clearly, the life he had led. Hence his obsession with the fact that he had fallen away and his begging God to help him never to fall away again. His difficulty with regard to faith was subjective: if he had failed once, could he be sure he would not fail again?

After his real conversion, Pascal's behavior became obsessively ascetic. The most probable explanation for this is his dogged determination that his body not entice him again away from the Lord. "His pursuit of saintliness was through pain, self-torture, renunciation of all life's consolations, . . . " writes Morris Bishop, "His ascetic practice was an act of conscious logic."[7] Pascal stripped his room of everything except the bare essentials, even for a time abandoning the use of a broom. He carried his

---

[7]Bishop, *Pascal*, 337.

own meals from the kitchen, refusing any domestic help. He always gave to any who asked alms of him, and, when he had no money left to give, he borrowed so as to give further. "His charity was very possibly ill-judged; it has the appearance of being performed because Pascal saw in it his duty, and not because those to whom he extended his bounty were very sore in need." So writes Jordan, and continues,

> It seems that the object which caused him to be charitable was not the good of those whom he assisted, but the benefit that he might gain from the conduct which he considered most became him. Thus he would borrow money, spend all that which he had, and busily occupy himself with the means of getting more, that the act which he considered right might be more frequent.[8]

His austerity extended even to unhealthily rebuking his married sister, Gilberte Périer, for allowing her children to embrace her—such a practice, he said "could only be injurious to them, . . . there were a thousand other ways in which one could show one's love to them."[9]

As his end drew near, and sickness was his lot, he said,

> Do not be sorry for me, sickness is the natural condition for Christians, because in that state one is as one should always be, that is, in suffering, illness, the deprivation of all good things and all pleasures of the senses, free from all passions, without ambition, without avarice, and in the continual expectation of death. Is it not thus that Christians should pass their lives? And is it not a great good fortune when one is by necessity in a state in which one ought properly to be?[10]

Later he adds, "Miserable as we are, powerless as we are, our friends won't aid us; we shall die alone."[11] Here is renunciation similar to that of Alissa of *Strait Is the Gate* by André Gide. She shares with Pascal the aloneness at the end, which is the product of what Morris Bishop calls an "ascetic practice which was an act of conscious logic." Her final words are, "I would like to die now, quickly, before realizing all over again how alone

---

[8]Jordan, *Blaise Pascal*, 137.

[9]Pascal, *Oeuvres complètes*, 24 (A.T.).

[10]Ibid., 32 (A.T.).

[11]Ibid., 1181 (A.T.).

I am.''[12] A hymn written many years ago (the writer wished to remain anonymous) captures so clearly the distinction between asceticism and the release of revelation:

> What has stripped the seeming beauty
> 　From the idols of the earth?
> Not a sense of right or duty,
> 　But the sight of peerless worth.
>
> Not the crushing of those idols,
> 　With its bitter void and smart;
> But the beaming of His beauty,
> 　The unveiling of His heart.
>
> Who extinguishes their taper
> 　Till they hail the rising sun?
> Who discards the garb of winter
> 　Till the summer has begun?
>
> 'Tis that look that melted Peter,
> 　'Tis that face that Stephen saw,
> 'Tis that heart that wept with Mary,
> 　Can alone from idols draw.

We cannot "discard the garb of winter till the summer has begun" without catching cold. But when the warmth of summer arrives, we long to lay aside our winter coat, which had seemed essential for protection through the cold winter months, but, once the warmth arrives, seems all at once an impediment, an embarrassment—an unnecessary load and chain. Pascal and Alissa tried to hasten the arrival of summer by throwing away their winter coats.

Pascal's final words, as he received the last sacrament, were: "May God never abandon me."[13] It seems the fear he expressed on the night of his true conversion continued with him, even to his deathbed. This is a sad note on which to end this chapter; but it is, alas, the true one.

---

[12]André Gide, *Romans, récits et soties, oeuvres lyriques,* intro. Maurice Nadeau, Bibliothèque de la Pléiade 135 (Paris: Éditions Gallimard, 1956) 595 (A.T.).

[13]Pascal, *Oeuvres complètes,* 34 (A.T.).

CHAPTER 7

The "Minds" of Pascal

————— // —————

What is surprising about the study of Pascal is to find evidence in his works of most of the "minds" to which I have referred up to this point, but regrettably not much that is simply and purely spiritual. Here I first examine in sequence incidences of various "minds," and then the exception.

THE MYSTIC MIND

The short section of the *Pensées* (*Thoughts*) entitled "Le Mystère de Jésus" ("The Mystery of Jesus"), since it is brief, is translated in its entirety and included in appendix B below. " 'The Mystery of Jesus,' " Brunschvig says, "defies all commentary. Nowhere, perhaps, does the unique and incomparable character of Christianity shine forth in a manner which is more deeply touching: the concentration around a real person of the highest and most universal feelings possible in the heart of man, the spirit of renunciation and the spirit of love."[1]

I contend that some of these thoughts (which comprise "The Mystery

——————————

[1] Blaise Pascal, *Pensées* (Paris: Garnier Frères, 1964) 337 (A.T.).

of Jesus''), being mystical and not spiritual, evoke a particular kind of feeling or sensation God-ward which colors the whole, and which is other than that produced by a simple reading of the Scriptures. Jean Mesnard unwittingly puts his finger on the key when he says, " 'Le Mystère de Jésus' is a meditation upon the agony on the Mount of Olives. In this intimate writing are revealed, in the most astonishing way, the deep religious sensitivity of Pascal and that powerful mystical imagination which transforms meditation into a dialogue, alone with Jesus.''[2] There is only one reliable way to approach the Scriptures—to read them with both mind and heart open for God, if He wishes, to reveal through the Spirit "things which eye saw not, and ear heard not, and which entered not into the heart of man, whatsoever things God prepared for them that love him" (1 Cor 2:9). The product of the "mystical imagination" of man will inevitably be misleading, whereas anything revealed of God through the Spirit will be true. I have selected several portions from "The Mystery of Jesus" where, I believe, the product of Pascal's imagination is particularly and perceptibly erroneous, and where the emotion evoked is unhealthy.

1. Jesus seeks at least some comfort from His three dearest friends, and they sleep. He begs them to support Him a little, and they leave Him with complete indifference, not having enough compassion to prevent them sleeping, even for a moment. (A.T.)

This theme dominates almost the first half* of "The Mystery of Jesus." It is altogether appropriate to observe the weaknesses and failures in men in general and in the disciples in particular, as they are portrayed in the Scriptures; but surely Pascal is overly derogatory towards them here, his objective being to emphasize the aloneness of Jesus. After all, these men had left all to follow Him, and, after Pentecost were to live their lives wholly for Him, most of them dying violent deaths as martyrs. In the garden they were mentally exhausted by all that had transpired during the immediately preceding days, and oppressed by what they feared was coming, for Jesus had told them of it on several occasions (Matt 16:21, 17:22, 20:17, Jn 14-16). They were not yet born of the Spirit "for the Spirit was not yet given

---

[2]Jean Mesnard, *Pascal,* trans. Claude Abraham and Marcia Abraham (Tuscaloosa AL: University of Alabama Press, 1969) 138.

*That is, sixty-two of 141 lines in the Bibliothèque de la Pléiade edition of Pascal's works.

because Jesus was not yet glorified" (Jn 7:39). What Pascal evidently missed was a little modifying phrase: "And when he rose up from his prayer, he came unto the disciples, and found them sleeping *for sorrow*" (Lk 22:45). Jesus was his disciples' very life: when He asked if they would leave Him even as all others were leaving, Peter replied, "Lord, to whom shall we go? Thou hast the words of eternal life. And we have believed and know that thou art the Holy One of God" (Jn 6:68). After He had risen, He appeared on the bank as Peter and the others were fishing fruitlessly, and when He let His identity be known, Peter dived over the side and swam to Him (Jn 21:1-14). There was no lack of devotion or love towards Him: on that fateful night they were *sleeping for sorrow*. It was as if they sensed what was coming, and were already mourning in advance—mental exhaustion, especially coupled with grief, may readily produce sleep.

> 2. Jesus will be in agony even until the end of the world: We must not sleep during that time. (A.T.)

The effect of this phrase is to evoke an upsurge of a certain kind of emotional, mystical, feeling God-ward. But is the first half true? Is "Jesus will be in agony even until the end of the world" a true statement? The Scriptures testify that it is not.

> For we have not a high priest that cannot be touched with the feeling of our infirmities; but one that hath been in all points tempted like as we are, yet without sin. (Heb 4:15)

It is evident that Jesus feels for us and with us, as we suffer. But His *agony*, the experience through which He passed to pay the price of sin, and to secure our salvation, was a single act, accomplished in history, which produced a specific effect:

> . . . he, when he had offered one sacrifice for sins for ever, sat down on the right hand of God; from henceforth expecting till his enemies be made the footstool of his feet. For by one offering he hath perfected for ever them that are sanctified. (Heb 10:12-14)

Although Jesus is called "a lamb . . . who was foreknown indeed before the foundation of the world" (1 Pet 1:19-20, indicating his willingness, before the world was, to go to the cross if man should subsequently fall into sin), and is seen, in eternity to come, as "a Lamb standing, as though it had been slain" (Rev 5:6, indicating that the marks of his suffering are indelible), nevertheless His *agony* neither extends continuously from eternity to eternity, nor is repeated during it: it was a historical event in time, clearly understandable to anyone who is inclined to enquire into its meaning. When it was over, Jesus cried out, "It is finished" (Jn 19:30).

Three days after the work was *finished,* he walked on the road to Emmaus with two disciples who did not recognize him, and said to them, "O foolish men, and slow of heart to believe in all that the prophets have spoken! Behooved it not the Christ to suffer these things, and to enter into his glory?" (Luke 24:25-26). Indeed, Isaiah had looked forward to this historic act, first describing it and then explaining the future resultant satisfaction of God's justice: "Thou [God] shalt make his [Christ's] soul an offering for sin, . . . he [God] shall see the travail of his [Christ's] soul, and shall be satisfied" (Isa 53:10-11). Then, prophesying as if he were looking back on the cross, he adds, "because he poured out his soul unto death" (Isa 53:12).

His agony is over. But that is no reason why we should sleep.

> 3. Jesus tears Himself away from His disciples in order to enter into His agony; we must tear ourselves away from our nearest and dearest so as to imitate Him. (A.T.)

One thinks at once of Thomas à Kempis's words: "Whoever is resolved to live an inward and spiritual life must, with Jesus, withdraw from the crowd. . . . It is commendable in a Religious to go abroad but seldom, to avoid being seen, and to have no desire to see men" (see above, p. 39). It is unnecessary to repeat here what was said earlier regarding mysticism; suffice to say only that often the deepest things are accomplished for God through Christians working together, and not alone. Indeed, there is a discipline in working with others that requires grace at a deeper level than may ever be experienced by one alone. Thus Paul worked with Barnabas, Silas, and Timothy; and Jesus exhorted us, "If two of you shall agree on earth as touching anything that they shall ask, it shall be done for them of my Father which is in heaven. For where two or three are gathered together in my name, there am I in the midst of them" (Matt 18:19). Withdrawing on occasion for a time of private prayer and meditation is, of course, right and beneficial, but ascetic *tearing away* is exaggerated; there is no indication that even the Lord Jesus did this. Matthew recorded that, in the garden, "he went forward a little, and fell on his face, and prayed, saying" (Matt 26:39). (Mark's and Luke's accounts are quite similar.) Indeed, even if He had *torn Himself away* to enter His agony, which He did not, that would be no justification for us to imagine we should do the same.

> 4. Comfort yourself, you would not seek me if you had not found me. . . . You would not seek me if you did not possess me. Therefore, be not troubled. (A.T.)

This is dangerous: it encourages an ignoble side of human nature. Don Juan, who loved the quest but was fearful of the limiting effect of finding, displays a common malady. For every one who genuinely wants to find spiritually there are many who enjoy the fascination of the search (there is a hunting instinct in man), but who back off when *arriving* becomes imminent.

The Scriptures do not say "Your seeking proves you have found me"; rather "Ask, and it shall be given you; seek, and ye shall find; knock, and it shall be opened unto you: for everyone that asketh receiveth; and he that seeketh findeth; and to him that knocketh it shall be opened" (Matt 7:7). In each of the three cases it is the promise of a future reward for a present action. Had Pascal said "Your seeking is proof that the Holy Spirit of God is drawing you," that would have been quite different.

Why did Pascal write this, which has been so warmly embraced by so many? I believe the key can be found in the last four words: "Therefore, be not troubled." After his second and real conversion Pascal lacked assurance and was constantly fearful he might fall away again. Telling himself that his seeking God was proof he possessed Him was comforting.

The memorial— mentioned in the last chapter—Pascal wrote on the night of his real conversion, also has a mystic connotation, not so much in its content as in the role the scrap of paper played. Pascal sewed it into the lining of his doublet, and later transferred it into the lining of the next doublet when the first wore out. Its inaccessibility indicates he did not keep it to read it, but rather for some sort of comfort he derived from having it always on his person, tangible evidence of an experience that represented his spiritual assurance. One cannot imagine Paul or any other biblical figure doing such a thing; it would never have occurred to them: their day-by-day walk by faith conveyed to them all the assurance they needed.

THE DESCARTES MIND

Whereas Descartes used his reason in his quest to prove the existence of God, Pascal used his to seek to prove both that God exists and that man should believe in Him—not a great difference. "The way of God, who disposes all things kindly, is to place religion in the mind through reasons and in the heart by grace,"[3] writes Pascal, and then elaborates as to the method of his apology for the Christian faith:

> Men despise religion; they hate it and fear it is true. In order to remedy this, one must begin by showing that religion is not contrary to reason, that it is venerable, and should be respected; then one must make it attractive so as to make good men wish it were true; and finally one must demonstrate that it is true.[4]

Pascal deplores the indifference of those who do not seek, and tries to frighten them into a change of heart:

> . . . this eternity exists, and death, which opens the door to it, and threatens them [the indifferent] every hour, must inevitably bring them, and soon, to face being either annihilated or miserable, without their knowing which of these eternities lays in store for them.[5]

His tactics become more menacing:

> Just imagine a number of men in chains, and all condemned to death, some being killed daily in full view of the others, while those who remain alive see their own condition in that of their fellows, and wait their turn looking at one another with sorrow and hopelessness. Such is a picture of the condition of man.[6]

Jonathan Edwards and his image of the spider evoke the same kind of emotion, but rather more forcefully:

> . . . the God that holds you over the pit of hell, much as one holds a spi-

---

[3]Blaise Pascal, *Oeuvres complètes. Texte établi et annoté par Jacques Chevalier*, Bibliothèque de la Pléiade 34 (Paris: Éditions Gallimard, 1954) 1090 (A.T.).

[4]Ibid., 1089 (A.T.).

[5]Ibid., 1171 (A.T.).

[6]Ibid., 1180 (A.T.).

der, or some loathsome insect, over the fire, abhors you, and is dreadfully provoked; his wrath towards you burns like fire. . . . You hang by a slender thread, with the flames of divine wrath flashing about it.[7]

Never does one find Jesus Christ or any of His disciples using such images and techniques as Pascal and Jonathan Edwards use here. From this one may deduce that such images and techniques are not a true representation of the mind and ways towards man of a God who is love. Statements such as these unfortunately expose Pascal to the barbs of Voltaire, who, ever on the lookout for a chink in the armor, accuses him of being a "sublime misanthropist."[8] On occasion, in his longing to persuade the atheist, Pascal descends to illustrations that are unseemly:

A virgin, why can she not bear a child? Does a hen not lay eggs without a cock? Who can distinguish the ones from the others? And who has told us that the hen cannot produce this seed as well as the cock?[9]

It would appear to be an oversight on Voltaire's part that he did not single out this statement for abuse also.*

Fundamentally, however, whereas Descartes's efforts to prove the existence of God were based on his ability to perceive perfection though he himself was imperfect, Pascal approaches the matter as a mathematician:

We know that there is such a thing as infinity, and are ignorant of its nature. As we know it to be false that numbers are finite, it is therefore true that there is an infinity in number. But we do not know what it is: it is not true that it is even, it is not true that it is odd; because the addition of one unit does not change its nature; however, it is a number and every number is either even or odd (which is true of every finite number). Thus one can know of assurety that there is a God without knowing what He is.[10]

[7]Ralph Turnbull, *Jonathan Edwards the Preacher* (Grand Rapids MI: Baker Book House, 1958) 61.

[8]Voltaire, *Lettres philosophiques* (Paris: Garnier Frères, 1962) 141 (A.T.).

[9]Pascal, *Oeuvres complètes*, 1182 (A.T.).

*In all fairness it should be mentioned that Pascal jotted down these *Thoughts* on random scraps of paper. Had he opportunity, which his early death prevented, to review and edit them, he may have changed much and eliminated some.

[10]Pascal, *Oeuvres complètes*, 1212 (A.T.).

But this does not advance matters much as it is still no proof that God does in fact exist. At this point Pascal proceeds "according to natural lights."

> If there is a God, He is infinitely incomprehensible, since, having neither parts nor limits, he has no affinity to us. We are therefore incapable of knowing either what He is or if He is. That being the case, who will dare undertake resolving this question? Certainly not we, who have no affinity to him.[11]

> God is or He is not. But which alternative shall we choose? Reason is powerless to decide anything here: an infinite chaos separates us. A game is being played at the extremity of this infinite distance in which either heads or tails will turn up. On which side will you place your bet? . . . Let us weigh the gain and loss in betting that God is. . . . If you win you win everything; if you lose you lose nothing.[12]

It would seem irrefutable, from this argument, that anyone who does not believe in the existence of God is a fool; yet, paradoxically, in practice the argument is impotent. One might note that there are so few readers of Pascal who attribute their conversion to him, a fact for which there must be a reason. Like Descartes, Pascal uses reason to lead the horse to the trough to drink; but Pascal then goes further and seeks to persuade his reader to take the *leap of faith,* and to accomplish this, he says, one must "renounce one's reason," something Camus refused to do, calling it— rightly I believe—a violation of intellectual integrity.*

It is this very article by Pascal on betting on the existence of God that prompts Voltaire to write,

> It is obviously false to say, "Not to bet that God exists is to bet that he doesn't"; for he who doubts and seeks enlightenment certainly does not bet either for or against. Moreover this article seems a little indecent and puerile; this idea of a game, of loss and gain, is not at all fitting when treating a subject of such gravity. Furthermore, the interest I have in believing a thing is no proof of the existence of that thing. . . . Your rea-

---

[11]Ibid., 1213 (A.T.).

[12]Ibid., 1214 (A.T.).

*See chap. 10, "The Leap of Faith," of my *The Spiritual Quest of Albert Camus* (Tuscaloosa AL: Portal Press, 1976).

soning would only have the effect of making atheists, if the voice of all nature did not cry out to us, with as much authority as these subtle arguments have weakness, that there is a God.[13]

It is indeed unfortunate that Pascal, through allowing his reason to trespass in spiritual things, should expose himself to being put in his place, and concerning those very spiritual things, by Voltaire.

THE MONTAIGNE MIND

"By the time a man knew Montaigne well enough to attack him," T. S. Eliot warned (see above, p. 50), "he would already be thoroughly infected by him." It is clear Pascal did make a thorough study of Montaigne, and was indeed "infected by him": "It is not in Montaigne," he said, "but in myself that I find all that I see in him."[14] Pascal understood and emulated Montaigne's style:

> The writing style of Epictetus, Montaigne, and Salomon de Tultie is the most effective, the most suggestive, continues longer in the memory, is the most often quoted, because it is entirely composed of thoughts that arise in the ordinary conversations of life."[15]

Salomon de Tultie is an anagram of Louis de Montalte which was the pseudonym Pascal adopted as author of the *Provincial Letters*. (It is thought he wished to use this same pseudonym for his apology for the Christian faith that he was preparing.) Madame Périer, Pascal's elder sister, may have composed this particular paragraph; it is nonetheless true, however, that there is common ground in the thought and style of Montaigne and Pascal.

In a number of instances Pascal comments, sometimes favorably and sometimes critically, on Montaigne's essays; and there are occasions where one finds thoughts that appear to have been lifted directly out of Montaigne's works. Bernard Jean and François Mouret suggest that "Pascal plagiarizes [from Montaigne] so much the more for having the better learned his lesson. And if, as did Descartes, he discards the book which taught him, it is because he also is a true disciple, and Montaigne ever the good

---

[13]Voltaire, *Lettres philosophiques*, 146 (A.T.).

[14]Pascal, *Oeuvres complètes*, 1104 (A.T.).

[15]Ibid., 1502 (A.T.).

teacher.''[16]

I said earlier (see above, p. 51) that Montaigne ''knows how to escape his soul's domination by living in his spirit (the spirit of the man which is in him). He proceeds out to the farthest limits of this spirit of the man in him, so as to be as free as possible from the disruptive, confused stirrings of his soul, and then politely but firmly turns his back on God and His Spirit, and, from this vantage point, becomes an inquisitive spectator of the inner workings of the human soul.'' Pascal does not, of course, ''politely but firmly turn his back on God and His Spirit''; but the very best of his work, the work which Christian and non-Christian alike appreciate the most, and of which we shall speak in the last section of this chapter, does not treat of the Scriptures, nor of God, except his infinite remoteness, but is written from the same sort of vantage point as Montaigne's, portraying man's place in the creation, the enigmas in his life, his psychological capacities and limitations.

THE AQUINAS MIND

Apart from the mind that is uniquely Pascalian, I have left Aquinas till last because it is here that the comparison is the most tenuous. The distinction (drawn in chapter 2, above) between those writings of Augustine that are spiritual and the writings of Aquinas that are intellectual is, I believe, valid. Any truth of God, which touches a person spiritually, evokes a response from the whole person; therefore, in expressing that truth, such a person will seek, spontaneously and probably unwittingly, to make the presentation convincing and acceptable. It is made convincing through eloquence (one senses that cheap language is unworthy and cannot convey such things), and acceptable by being presented in such a way as to be spiritually relevant and appealing, which is accomplished through grace.

Pascal knew all about eloquence: it is, he said, ''a painting of thought.'' Then he added, ''There has to be both what is pleasant and what is true in it; but what is pleasant must be drawn from the true.''[17] Yet in so much of

---

[16]Bernard Jean and François Mouret, *Montaigne, Descartes, and Pascal* (Manchester GB: Manchester University Press, 1971) vi (A.T.).

[17]Pascal, *Oeuvres complètes,* 1099 (A.T.).

the latter part of the *Thoughts*,*there is often little evidence of eloquence or grace, and it seems as if spiritual matters are treated almost mathematically. "In the state in which Pascal left his apology," M. des Granges asked, "did he himself know what use he would make of all these thoughts, some of which he would have eliminated, and others whose form and place he would without doubt have changed? . . . And if Pascal could see the reproductions of his *Thoughts*, would he not be surprised to find in them many passages which he would consider an almost algebraic notation of an idea, an objection, or a rejoinder, without his being able any longer to perceive their significance or place?"[18]

Following are some random examples of the above, selected one from each section of the Brunschvicg edition.

1. The fundamentals of the Christian Religion.

We understand nothing of the works of God, if we do not accept as a principle that He wanted to blind some and give enlightenment to the others.[19]

This is cold logic, and simply not a true representation of the mind of God (see above, pp. 66-67, on predestination). Seeking to excuse Pascal, some attribute this *thought* to the Jansenist influence on his life.

2. Perpetuity.

No religion other than our own has taught that man is born in sin, no sect of philosophers has said this: therefore none has declared the truth.
No sect or religion has always existed on the earth, except the Christian religion.[20]

This would not convince adherents of other religions or atheists, all of whom seek to explain man's condition in other terms than sin. Also Chris-

---

*In the "Brunschvicg edition," particularly from the "The Mystery of Jesus" to the end, which comprises the principal section where Pascal treats the Scriptures. Blaise Pascal, *Oeuvres complètes, publiées suivant l'ordre chronologique, avec documents, complémentaires, introductions et notes*, ed. Léon Brunschvicg, P. Boutroux, and F. Gazier, 14 vols. (Paris, 1904–1914).

[18]Pascal, *Pensées*, vii (A.T.).

[19]Ibid., 220 (A.T.).

[20]Ibid., 229 (A.T.).

tianity only exists as a movement since the day of Pentecost. It was preceded by Judaism which, as a religion, exists since the exodus of the
children of Israel from Egypt into the desert.

3. Topology.

> *Proof of the two Testaments at one and the same time.* To prove the two
> at one stroke, we only have to see if the prophecies of the one are fulfilled
> in the other. To examine the prophecies we must understand them. For,
> if we believe that they only have one meaning, it is certain that the Mes-
> siah has not come; but if they have two meanings it is certain that He came
> in Jesus Christ. Thus the whole problem is to know if they have two
> meanings.
>
> That the Scripture has two meanings, which Jesus Christ and the apostles
> have given, is demonstrated by the following proofs.
>
> 1. Proof by the Scripture itself;
> 2. Proof by the Rabbis: Moses Maimonides says that it has two aspects,
>   and that the prophets only prophesied concerning Jesus Christ;
> 3. Proof by the Kabbala;
> 4. Proof by the mystical interpretation which the Rabbis themselves give
>   to the Scripture. etc.[21]

Were this section developed and presented in a more interesting style
it might carry some weight, although the central hypothesis is questionable. There are surely many prophecies regarding Christ that have only one
meaning, namely, that which is fulfilled in Him, for example, the prophecy in Isaiah 53 regarding His sufferings, or the prophecy at Micah 5:2 of
His birthplace: "But thou, Bethlehem Ephrathah, which art little to be
among the thousands of Judah, out of thee shall one come forth unto me
that is to be ruler of Israel; whose goings forth are from old, from everlasting."

4. The Prophecies.

> *Prophecies*— Amos and Zechariah: They have sold the just one, and for
> that they will never be recalled. —Jesus Christ betrayed.
>
> They shall no longer remember Egypt: see Is. 43:16, 17, 18, 19; Jer. 23:6,
> 7.
>
> *Prophecies*—The Jews will be scattered abroad in every direction. Is.
> 27:6. —A new law. Jer. 31:32.

---

[21]Ibid., 244 (A.T.).

Malachi. *Grotius.*—The second temple glorious.—Jesus Christ will come. Haggai 2:7, 8, 9, 10.
The calling of the Gentiles. Joel 2:28. Hosea 2:24. Deut. 32:21. Malachi 1:11.[22]

I do not believe it is possible to discern Pascal's purpose in linking these concepts and passages, if, indeed, he had any intention to link them. They may represent separate thoughts, each of which he intended to develop independently.

5. The Proofs of Jesus Christ.

If all the Jews had been converted by Jesus Christ, we would only have witnesses who were suspect. And if they had all been exterminated, we would not have any witnesses at all.[23]

This is a good example of what I call Pascal's "equation mind"—a statement followed by a counterbalancing antithesis or corollary. The *thought* is catchy, but is it anything beyond that? Surely it would be nearer the truth to say, "All the Jews could not have been converted by Jesus Christ because He foresaw that some of them would kill Him; thus, if all the Jews were converted, it could only have been by someone other than Jesus Christ." One can almost hear Gide complaining that such talk gives "a splitting headache and the desire to go out into the fresh air to walk it off." (See above, p. 55.)

6. The Miracles.

Miracle. —It is an effect which exceeds the natural power of the means one employs to perform it; and a non-miracle is an effect which does not exceed the natural power of the means employed to perform it. Thus, those who heal by invoking the devil do not perform a miracle; since that does not exceed the natural power of the devil.[24]

This is no more than an elaborate, and rather misleading, way of stating a definition—that, to Pascal, the word *miracle* meant something done by God.

---

[22]Ibid., 285 (A.T.).

[23]Ibid., 285 (A.T.).

[24]Morris Bishop, *Pascal. The Life of a Genius* (New York: Reynal and Hitchcock, 1936) 291.

This section has been rather depressing. I set out to seek to prove that, like Aquinas, Pascal is often intellectual rather than spiritual in his exposition of the Scriptures. I find myself of necessity going beyond and accusing Pascal of erroneous or misleading thinking—a charge to which Aquinas, I believe, would be much less vulnerable.

THE PASCALIAN MIND

The thoughts of Pascal reappear in Leibniz, Kant, Schopenhauer, Nietzche, Darwin, Taine, Newman, William James. From about 1885 onward French thought became aware of its own sympathy with Pascal. Rationalism gave way to a spiritualist philosophy of intuition. Especially was Bergson imbued with Pascalian thought. "Bergson," says C. G. Amoit, "is carried on the stream of Pascal as a boat floats on a broad river."

Since 1660 the evolution of humanity has proved [Pascal] right with a vengeance. The rationalist humanism and the optimism of the century of enlightenment, science, international organizations have ended in fraudulent bankruptcies. All that counts in psychology from Nietzsche to Proust, from Stendhal to Dostoyevski, from Kafka to Malraux and Camus, develops, elaborates and extends the intuitions of Pascal. It seems that all the great voices echo his own.[25]

Of the fifteen authors in these two quotations, would any except Newman and Dostoyevski claim to be believing Christians? Camus and Kafka show sensitivity to spiritual issues, while, at the other end of the spectrum, Nietzsche is violently antipathetic towards Christianity, and assaults it in a manner exceeding even that of Voltaire. It is probable that all these authors totally discounted the area of the *Thoughts* (treated in the section immediately preceding this) in which Pascal expounds the Scriptures. The common ground of all of them is psychological, and it is here that Pascal's genius shines the most brightly. With an extraordinary precision and economy of words he gave expression to the universal psychological experience of man in relation to society, personal happiness, and so forth.

  1. Society.

---

[25]Jean Steinmann, *Pascal*, trans. Martin Turnell (New York: Harcourt Brace and World Inc., 1965) 242.

No one speaks of us in our presence as he does in our absence. The relationships between men are based only on this mutual deceit; and few friendships would last if each knew what his friend said about him in his absence, even though he spoke at that time sincerely and without passion.

Thus man is nothing but disguise, a lie and hypocrisy both toward himself and with regard to others. Therefore he does not want to be told the truth. He avoids telling it to others; and all these dispositions, so far removed from justice and reason, have their natural roots in his heart.[26]

2. Personal happiness.

Let each man examine his thoughts—he will find them entirely occupied with the past and the future. We hardly ever think about the present at all, and,if we do think of it, it is only to take light from it to make ready for the future. The present is never our objective: the past and the present are our means; the future alone is our end. Thus we never live, but we hope to live; and, as we are always getting ready to be happy, it is inevitable that we shall never be so.[27]

3. The heart's relationship to the head.

The heart has its reasons of which reason is totally unaware.[28]

4. The Universe.

The visible world is no more than an imperceptible dot in the ample bosom of nature . . . which is an infinite sphere whose center is everywhere and circumference nowhere. . . . What is man in relation to nature? A Nothing when compared to infinity, an Everything when compared to nothing—half way between nothing and everything. Since he is infinitely removed from comprehending the extremes, the ultimate end of things and their origin are hopelessly hidden from him in an impenetrable secret—he is equally incapable of seeing the Nothing whence he was formed, and the infinity in which he is engulfed.[29]

Man is not more than a reed, the weakest thing in nature; but he is a think-

---

[26]Pascal, *Oeuvres complètes,* 1125 (A.T.).

[27]Ibid., 1132 (A.T.).

[28]Ibid., 1221 (A.T.).

[29]Ibid., 1103 (A.T.).

ing reed. It doesn't need the whole universe to arm itself to crush him: a vapor, a drop of water suffices to kill him. But if the universe should crush him, man would still be more noble than what kills him because he knows he is dying, and the Universe knows nothing of the advantage it has over him. Our whole dignity, therefore, consists in thought.[30]

How much loftier is the Pascalian notion that thought is the measure of our dignity than the Cartesian (of Descartes) that our thinking proves our existence.

Our theme here is not psychological, however, but rather the roles that reason and revelation play in the minds of our authors. The impression would be false if the reader were to deduce from what we have written so far that a complete representation of what Pascal thought about these matters is to be found in the section on *The Descartes mind* concerning the wager (that God exists). The fact is, Pascal understood very clearly the necessity of revelation:

> The last step reason can take is to recognize that there is an infinity of things which are beyond it; it is but feeble if it doesn't go as far as seeing this. And if natural things go beyond reason, what will one say of supernatural?[31]

> Faith tells clearly what the senses do not tell, but not the contrary of what they see. It is above, and not contrary to them.[32]

> *St. Augustine.* —Reason would never submit if it did not judge that there are occasions on which it should submit. It is therefore right for it to submit, when it judges that it should.[33]

> If we submit everything to reason, our religion will have nothing mysterious and supernatural about it. If we offend the principles of reason, our religion will be absurd and ridiculous.[34]

> It is the heart and not the reason which experiences God. This is what is meant by faith: God sensed by the heart and not by the reason.[35]

---

[30]Ibid., 1156 (A.T.).

[31]Ibid., 1219 (A.T.).

[32]Ibid., 1218 (A.T.).

[33]Ibid. (A.T.).

[34]Ibid., 1089 (A.T.).

[35]Ibid., 1222 (A.T.).

Do not be surprised if you see simple people believe without reasoning. God imparts to them love of Him and hatred of themselves. He inclines their hearts to believe. Man will never believe with a saving and real faith unless God inclines his heart; and he will believe from the moment that God inclines it. David knew this well: *Inclina cor meum, Deus, in . . .* (Incline my heart . . . , Ps 119:36).[36]

How can all of this be reconciled with the cold logic of the wager (the bet that God exists) in the previous section on *The Descartes mind?* Pascal answers:

Those to whom God has imparted religion through a sense in the heart are very fortunate, and really properly convinced. But to those who do not have it in this way we can only give it by reasoning until God gives it to them by a sense in the heart, without which faith is only human and is useless for salvation.[37]

This goes quite a long way towards justifying the former passage on the wager, except that here he recognizes that the horse can be led to the trough, but cannot be made to drink, whereas there he tried to force the issue by pressingly advocating the *leap of faith* (above, p. 82).

But this last series of quotations is not greatly different in style from the group which immediately precedes it—if the former group deals with man's psychological relationships, these latter could be called a psychology of Redemption. The question arises whether all Pascal's spiritual observations are cast in this analytic vein or whether there is evidence anywhere in his work of homiletic appeal. His *Lettres provinciales* (*Provincial Letters*), which he wrote in defense of Antoine Arnauld and against the excesses of the Jesuits and their casuistry, are brilliant in their wit, humor, satire of ideas, and irony of expression. Morris Bishop writes that

Pascal's style in the Provincial Letters is marked also by eloquence, a quality suggested, but hardly attained, in his earlier work. At need, the tone of his polemic rises from the realistic or the ironic to the nobly impassioned. He finds grave, sonorous words for his thought; the clauses lengthen, to the cadence of a resonant voice half heard; the sentences fall into those rhythmic patters which seem proper to anger, scorn, or grief.

---

[36]Ibid., 1344 (A.T.).

[37]Ibid., 1222 (A.T.).

But nothing declamatory, nothing orotund. "True eloquence disdains eloquence, true morality disdains morality," he wrote. Pascal, in the *provinciales*, introduced into French prose the eloquence which disdains eloquence.[38]

But was this work truly spiritual? Most in Port Royal were delighted to have a new champion; but the more spiritually perceptive among them, and particularly M. Singlin and Mère Angélique (the sister of Antoine Arnauld whom Pascal sought to defend), were offended and apprehensive. "Silence," said Mère Angélique, "would have been fairer and more agreeable to God, who is better appeased by tears of penitence than by the eloquence which beguiles more people than it converts."[39] Her words were prophetic—The *Provincial Letters* fascinated the general public, but infuriated the Jesuits and enemies of Jansenism, hastening the downfall of Port Royal. It is interesting to note that it was Pelagianism, which earlier drew Augustine off the spiritual ground that was properly his, that Pascal attacked here.

Is there then any truly spiritual work from the pen of Pascal which is also marked by "eloquence," as Morris Bishop defines that word when he uses it in relation to the *Provincial Letters?* One could cite certain exhortatory letters which Pascal wrote to Mlle de Roannez, or his *Prayer for the good use of sicknesses,* which latter however, is rather pietistic (under the guise of prayer, preaching to himself and others things which God knows well, instead of actually praying)—a far cry from the simple, healthy pragmatism of the apostle Paul: "There was given to me a thorn in the flesh, a messenger from Satan to buffet me, that I should not be exalted overmuch. Concerning this thing I besought the Lord thrice, that it might depart from me. And he said unto me, My grace is sufficient for thee: for my power is made perfect in weakness. Most gladly therefore will I rather glory in my weaknesses, that the power of Christ may rest upon me." (2 Cor 12:7-9)

There remains, however, the quite unusual little work *Concerning the conversion of a sinner,** that traces the upward saga of a soul whom God is touching. Critics suggest that the expression of emotions in this work

---

[38]Bishop, *Pascal,* 254.

[39]Ibid., 227.

*My translation of this little work is included below, in appendix B.

seems to be an exact description of Pascal's state of mind just prior to his real conversion in 1654, and attribute this work to him at that date. I contend that in his condition, as described by his sister Jacqueline at that time—"incessantly stung by his conscience," "[feeling] completely abandoned by God," "[believing] he was merely making an intellectual struggle to find God," "[assailed by temptations] to resist God's grace" (see above, p. 69)—it would have been impossible for him to have written in this way, that virtually breathes peace. Also, this work is different from any other by Pascal in that one is drawn along by the author into the sensation of the experience described, rather than viewing principles from the objective stance of a bystander. To the translator this work presents problems quite contrary to those usually encountered in Pascal. With all this, it is no surprise to read in the Bibliothèque de la Pléiade edition of Pascal's works that this little piece was at first attributed to Jacqueline Pascal: indeed the style is quite similar to that of her letter cited above (p. 69). It is surprising that, since the publication of Abbé Bossut's work on Pascal in 1779, more than 100 years following *Concerning the conversion,* this work has been ascribed to Blaise Pascal. Matthew 13:12 asserts that "Whosoever hath, to him shall be given, and he shall have abundance: but whosoever hath not, from him shall be taken away even that which he hath"—right and true in spiritual things, but unfortunate here.

CHAPTER 8

Jean-Jacques Rousseau

———— // ————

   Jean-Jacques Rousseau was born at Geneva, Switzerland, during June 1712. His mother died a few days after his birth, and he and his elder brother were raised by an aunt, Suzanne Rousseau, and a nursemaid. His father Isaac, a watchmaker who had been forced to take up this occupation as a consequence of financial exigency and the loss of social position, loved books. Isaac read novels and historical and moral works to his son, and, though such instruction was hardly formal or disciplined, he did inculcate in Jean-Jacques a voracious appetite as a reader. His Aunt Suzanne and the nursemaid coddled the boys, seeking to compensate them for the loss of their mother. Speaking of his early education, and the influence of the context in which he was raised, Jean-Jacques later wrote, "I felt before thinking." This sensitivity was always to precede and govern his intellectual activity.

   In 1722 Isaac Rousseau left Geneva and took up residence at Nyon: he had fought a duel and was obliged to leave his hometown, being threatened with imprisonment if he remained. Jean-Jacques, with his cousin, was boarded out with a Calvinist pastor, Lambercier, at Bossey near Geneva, where life in the country captivated him. The pastor continued Jean-Jacques's formal education but without much pressure on the student. Jean-Jacques's memories of his childhood both in Geneva and at Bossey were happy ones. Again, in the pastor's wife, he was blessed with an affectionate and considerate woman who sought to fill the parental gap in his life.

In 1724, when he was still thirteen, Jean-Jacques was employed for a brief time in a clerk's office in Geneva; but he was soon dismissed because of his "ineptitude," whereupon he was apprenticed to an engraver with whom he also went to live. Then his life changed abruptly. The brutality of his master and employer had the effect of disgusting him with an occupation which otherwise "in itself did not displease him." He submitted to the discipline, however, until a further incident dramatically altered the course of his life.

It was the custon to shut the city gates of Geneva at a certain hour each night. On two occasions Jean-Jacques arrived late, and the following morning was severly reprimanded. On the second occasion he was warned that the consequences would be most serious if he was late a third time. One day, after foraging in the countryside, and when he was still about half a mile from the city wall, he and his friends heard the signal that warned the gate was about to be shut. He ran as fast as he could and was within twenty yards when the drawbridge was raised.

> In the first excess of grief, I flung myself on the bank and gnawed at the earth. My companions, laughing at their misfortune, made up their minds on the spot what they would do. I made up mine also; but it was quite different from theirs; and the following day, when the gates of the city were opened and my friends went in, I said goodbye to them for ever.[1]

Jean-Jacques was just sixteen. He went to Annecy where he was received by a certain Mme. de Warens who virtually adopted him, taught him the ways of the world and later took him as her lover. She sent him first to a religious institution in Turin where he renounced Protestantism. He returned to Annecy and, over many years, continued his relationship with Mme. de Warens whom, as she was considerbly older, he called "maman."

In 1745 he took as mistress an illiterate laundress, Thérèse Levasseur, by whom he had five children, each of whom he sent to an orphange shortly after birth, all the while protesting that he was a good Christian man and that this was best for his children since his busy life as an author left him little time to take adequate care of them. Towards the end of his life, Rousseau married Thérèse; but in the meantime he had several affairs with la-

---

[1]Jean-Jacques Rosseau, *Confessions*, ed. Jacques Voisine (Paris: Garnier Frères, 1964) 45 (A.T.).

dies of distinction. He circulated among such famous writers as Diderot and Voltaire with whom he was not popular, and towards whom— indeed towards society in general—he developed a persecution complex during his latter years.

Rousseau wrote voluminously, most notably on politics—*The Social Contract*; on himself—*Confessions*; on romantic love—*La Nouvelle Héloise* (or *Julie*); on education— *Emile*. In this latter work Rousseau devoted a whole section—"The Profession of Faith of a Priest of Savoy"— to his ideas on religion. By following successive extracts from this work we shall now study Rousseau's notion of the distiction between reason and revelation.

> I was in that attitude of uncertainty and doubt which Descartes declares necessary for the pursuit of truth. . . . I kept saying to myself: "I love truth, I seek it, I cannot recognize it; let it be revealed to me, and I will remain firm in my acceptance of it."[2]

The church in which he was born offered little help—it was an institution which

> decides everything, which permits no doubts, the rejection of a single belief made me reject all the rest, and the impossibility of admitting so many absurd teachings turned me also against those others which were reasonable. By telling me, "Believe everything," they prevented me from believing anything, and I no longer knew what to accept.[3]

He consulted the philosophers, but

> found them all proud, assertive, dogmatic, even in their so-called skepticism, not recognizing their ignorance on any subject, proving nothing, mocking one another; and this mutual contempt, common to all, seemed to me the only point on which all are right.[4]

"Where is the philosopher," he asks, "who, for his own glory, would not readily deceive mankind?"[5] He realizes that, far from ridding him of his

---

[2]Jean-Jacques Rosseau, *The Creed of a Priest of Savoy*, trans. Arthur Beattie (New York: Frederick Ungar, 1956) 3.

[3]Ibid., 4.

[4]Ibid., 4.

[5]Ibid., 5.

doubts,

> philosophers would only multiply those which tormented me, and would
> resolve none of them. I took then another guide, and I said to myself: Let
> us consult the inner light; it will lead me astray less than philosophers
> lead me astray.[6]

Now he has a basis upon which to build; and it is no different from the
first principle he discovered in his youth: "I felt before thinking."

> I know only that the truth is in things and not in my mind which judges
> them, and that the less I put of my own in the judgments that I make con-
> cerning them, the surer I am of approaching the truth: thus my rule of
> trusting feeling more than reason is confirmed by reason itself.[7]

He perceives that the movement of matter requires a will that origi-
nated that movement, and that "the movement of matter according to certain laws reveals . . . an intelligence."[8] Thus he comes to believe

> that the world is governed by a powerful and wise will; I see it, or rather
> I feel it. . . . This being who has will and power, this being active in him-
> self, this being finally, whatever he may be, who moves the universe and
> governs all things, I call him God. . . . I perceive God everywhere in his
> works; I feel him within me; I see him all about me; but as soon as I seek
> to contemplate him in myself, as soon as I wish to seek where he is, what
> he is, what is his substance, he escapes me and my troubled mind per-
> ceives nothing more.[9]

This is a most promising and spiritual beginning. "That which is known
of God is manifest in them; for God manifested it unto them," Paul said.
"For the invisible things of him since the creation of the world are clearly
seen, being perceived through the things that are made, even his everlasting power and divinity" (Rom 1:19-20). But not only is the priest's perception of God in the creation quite in accord with Scripture, his notion of
man's place in the creation harmonizes also: "What is man, that thou art

---

[6]Ibid., 6.

[7]Ibid., 11.

[8]Ibid., 16.

[9]Ibid., 19, 20.

mindful of him?," the psalmist enquired. "For thou has made him but little lower than God, and crownest him with glory and honor" (Psalm 8:4-5). "What is so ridiculous about believing that everything is made for me," asks the priest, "if I am the only one who knows how to consider everything in relation to himself? It is therefore true that man is the king of nature, at least on this earth where he dwells."[10]

But while "animals are happy, their king alone is wretched."[11] His misery stems from the fact that he

> is not one; I will, and I do not will, I feel myself at the same time slave and free; I see the good, I love it, and yet I do evil; I am active when I listen to reason, passive when my passions lead me astray; and my worst torment, when I yield, is to feel that I might have resisted. . . . I have always the strength to will, but not always the strength to carry out my will. When I yield to temptations, I act according to the impulsion of external objects. When I reproach myself with that weakness, I listen only to my will. I am a slave by my vices, and free by my remorse.[12]

The words are different, but the perception is identical to that of Paul when he describes the sinful nature of man: "For I know that in me, that is, in my flesh, dwelleth no good thing: for to will is present with me, but to do that which is good is not. For the good which I would I do not: but the evil which I would not, that I practise." (Rom 7:18-19) "Man, seek no more the author of evil;" says the priest, "that author is yourself."[13]

He grasps not only the essence of man's relationship to God—"We are free only because he [God] wants us to be free, and his inexplicable substance is to our souls what our souls are to our bodies"[14]—but also man's own constitution (body, soul, and spirit).

> Conscience is the voice of the soul, passions are the voice of the body. Is it astonishing that often these two tongues contradict one another? And then which should you heed? Too often reason deceives us; we have only

---

[10]Ibid., 21.

[11]Ibid., 22.

[12]Ibid., 23, 25.

[13]Ibid., 28.

[14]Ibid., 34.

too often acquired the right to challenge it. Conscience, on the contrary, never deceives us; it is the true guide of man; it is to the soul what instinct is to the body.[15]

Conscience! Conscience! divine instinct, immortal and celestial voice . . . without you, I feel nothing in me which raises me above the beasts.[16]

Hitherto the "profession of faith" could hardly have been more promising and spiritually valid. It is as if the next logical step would have been to consider Jesus Christ and his claim to be the only-begotten Son of God, and the Savior of man; but this is not at all Rousseau's objective here, for this work is not an honest quest, as it appears thus far, but a carefully developed thesis with a specific end in view. It is at this point that the artifice becomes apparent. He clearly specifically refrains even from mentioning the name of Jesus Christ (except in a footnote) until he has first ridiculed the principle of revelation and glorified his reason. Then he pays two tangential compliments to Jesus Christ, a kind of sop to his conscience, before moving quickly on to describe his own comfortable, innocuous, deistic belief.

If he is to attack Revelation it can only be because it is contrary to reason; thus he must first establish the validity of his reason.

It is useless . . . to cry to me, "Make your reason yield." He who deceives me can say as much to me; I must have reasons if my reason is to give assent. [An echo of Pascal.] When I believe what a man says, it is not because he says it, but because he proves it. The testimony of men is, then, in the last analysis only that of my reason itself, and adds nothing to the natural means which God has given me to know the truth.[17]

There only remains to set the stage for this dialogue between reason and revelation:

If natural religion is insufficient, it is by the obscurity which it leaves in the great truths which it teaches to us: it is up to revelation to teach us these truths in such a way that the human mind may grasp them, to bring them within its reach, to make it understand them so that it may believe

---

[15]Ibid., 36.

[16]Ibid., 43.

[17]Ibid., 55.

them. . . . The God whom I worship is not a God of darkness; he has not endowed me with an understanding in order to forbid me to use it. To tell me to make my reason submit is to insult its creator.[18]

Then follows what I describe as the fruit of a ''fit of petulance,'' this ridiculous dialogue in which each interlocutor appears to be trying to outdo the other in arrogance and belligerence. Had this been at a higher level it might have served to demonstrate that any attempt to prove the principle of revelation without focusing it upon the one who is at the center of the universe, Jesus Christ, is bound to be a fruitless occupation.

SPOKESMAN FOR REVELATION— Reason teaches you that the whole is greater than the part; but I teach you, in God's name, that it is the part which is greater than the whole.

SPOKESMAN FOR REASON—And who are you to dare tell me that God contradicts himself? And in whom should I prefer to believe, in him who teaches me by my reason eternal truths, or in you who announce to me in his name an absurdity?

REVELATION—In me, for my teaching is more positive; and I am going to prove to you irrefutably, that it is he who sends me.

REASON— What! you will prove to me that it is God who sends you to give evidence against him? And what will be the nature of your proofs to convince me that it is more certain that God speaks to me through your mouth than through the understanding which he has given me?

REVELATION—The understanding which he has given you! Petty and vain man! As if you were the first impious person who is misled by his reason corrupted by sin!

REASON—Man of God, you would not be the first rascal, either, who offers his arrogance as proof of his mission.

REVELATION—What! Philosophers are insulting, too!

REASON—Sometimes, when saints set them the example.

REVELATION—Oh! I have the right to say such things; I speak for God.

REASON—It would be good to show your credentials before using your privilege.

REVELATION—My credentials are authentic; the earth and the heavens will

---

[18]Ibid., 60.

testify for me. Follow my reasongs, I beg you.

This is about one-third of the dialogue. This excerpt is sufficient to give an idea of the level of this conversation that ends for the spokesman for revelation with his calling the spokesman for reason a "minion of the demon."

Now the deed is done; revelation is ridiculed— or so Rousseau thought, and it is safe to doff his cap perfunctorily to Jesus Christ:

> When Plato depicts his imaginary just man covered with all the opprobrium of crime, and worthy of all the rewards of virtue, he is describing, trait by trait, Jesus Christ; the resemblance is so striking that all the church fathers felt it, and it is not possible to be mistaken about it. . . . If the life and death of Socrates are those of a sage, the life and death of Jesus are those of a god. Shall we say that the gospel story is the free invention of a lively imagination? My friend, this is not the sort of thing one invents; and the facts of Socrates' life, which no one doubts, are less well attested than those of Jesus Christ's.

Rousseau even goes so far as to eulogize the gospel, secure in his confidence in reason to reject it afterwards on account of what he regards as inconsistencies:

> The Gospel has such great, such striking, and such inimitable characteristics of truth that the inventor of it would be even more astonishing than his hero. Nonetheless, the same gospel is full of unbelievable things, of things which repel the reason, and which it is impossible for any reasonable man to imagine or to admint.[19]

"What is one to do in the midst of these contradictions?," enquires the priest, and then concludes,

> Be always modest and circumspect . . . ; respect in silence what one could neither reject nor understand, and humble yourself before the great Being who alone knows the truth.

The priest feels satisfied that he has justified the position he has reached, which he calls "involuntary skepticism." He regards

all religions as so many salutary institutions which prescribe in each

---

[19]Ibid., 73, 74.

country a uniform way of honoring God by public worship, and which can all have their reasons in the climate, the government, the spirit of the people, or in some other local cause which makes one preferable to the other, according to time and place. I believe them all good when in them one serves God fittingly.[20]

And thus we reach a sterile, innocuous end: How can all religions, which are different, be true? But then again Rousseau does not claim that they are all true, just that they are good, and this after what had seemed to be a promising and spiritual beginning.

Conclusion

It was a singular honor for the writer of Revelation to be the one through whom should be conveyed to the church the prophecies and revelations regarding the conclusion of this age and the dispositions for the age to come and for eternity. When he set himself to commit these visions to writing, the first words which came to him, which encompass all that is to follow, are profoundly significant: "The Revelation of Jesus Christ" (Rev 1:1).

Essentially Christianity is just that—no more, no less. After all, "in him [Jesus Christ] were all things created, in the heavens and upon the earth, things visible and things invisible, whether thrones or dominions or principalities or powers; all things have been created through him, and unto him; and he is before all things, and in him all things consist" (Col 1:16-17). How then is it possible really to comprehend the significance of any *thing* if its relationship to Him is not perceived?

When Descartes, after all his mental gyrations, triumphantly declares the existence of God, he has not really accomplished anything, for the Scripture answers him: "Thou believest that God is one; thou doest well: the demons also believe and shudder" (James 2:19). It almost seems that the devils are more in touch with reality, and, in a certain sense, in a clearer position spiritually, than Descartes—this knowledge at least provokes fear in them, but, sadly, a certain arrogance in him. For all that T. S. Eliot says (see above, p. 23) it is not possible to move logically step by step and arrive at the revelation of Jesus Christ. Logic seeks to move in from the periphery to the center, but is impotent to make the final "leap," as Pascal's "wager" proves conclusively (see above, p. 82).

Through his perception of things (the creation) man can never come to the revelation of Jesus Christ; but through the revelation of Jesus Christ he comes to understand the essential place of all things. Jesus told His disciples how they could receive this revelation: "For this is the will of my Father, that everyone that beholdeth the Son, and believeth on him, should have eternal life; and I will raise him up at the last day'' (Jn 6:40). The Greek verb θεωρέω *theōreō,* translated here "beholdeth," means "to gaze/ look on, as a spectator." Only when what is seen is appropriated by faith is there revelation. Another Greek verb, βλέπω *blepō,* indicates "to contemplate earnestly"; and a third verb, ὁράω *horaō,* introduces the concept of perception by a discerning mind. The differences between these three are rather clearly seen in the following passage regarding an incident at the tomb on the day of resurrection:

> Peter therefore went forth, and the other disciple [John], and they went toward the tomb. And they ran both together: and the other disciple outran Peter, and came first to the tomb; and stooping and looking in, he seeth [*blepō*] the linen cloths lying; yet entered he not in. Simon Peter therefore also cometh, following him, and entered into the tomb; and he beholdeth [*theōreō*] the linen cloths lying, and the napkin, that was upon his head, not lying with the linen cloths, but rolled up in a place by itself. Then entered in therefore the other disciple also, who came first to the tomb, and he saw [*horaō*], and believed. (Jn 20:3-8)

It is in man's power to go beyond gazing as a spectator to "contemplating earnestly" with an enquiring heart, which corresponds to "asking" and "seeking" (Matt 7:7). Anyone who does this will receive and find, in God's time. Those who knew Him on this earth could "contemplate earnestly" His actual life, and some were given to perceive: "Again on the morrow John [the Baptist] was standing, and two of his disciples; and he looked [*blepō*] upon Jesus as he walked, and saith, Behold, the Lamb of God!" (Jn 1:35-36). Today His life can be contemplated in the Gospels, and, in measure, in those in whom He lives. In His time, God gives certainty as to who He is; and a relationship begins which will never end.

Augustine sought Him earnestly. In his latter days Aquinas must have felt a dissatisfaction and a longing for more, which was clearly satisfied. Pascal, we know, was desperate, and set all else aside in his quest. All these received revelation of Jesus Christ. Jean-Jacques Rousseau, despite all his protestations to the contrary, and his apparent spiritual sensitivity, was not a candidate for the revelation of Jesus Christ (at least not in the *Profession of faith of a Priest of Savoy*). He obviously wished to hold Jesus Christ at arm's length, and arranged things so that paying Him compliments would keep Him there. On the surface of it, Paul appears to be an exception, and something of an enigma; but appearances are often deceptive, and an offensive exterior can be hiding a heart in agony and turmoil. And such was without doubt the condition of Paul as, night and day, he was unable to escape that face as of an angel, and the gracious Christ-like words, which were Stephen's as he died (see above, p. 3).

Revelation cannot be induced; it is not necessarily given in response to a "decision" being made; it cannot be attained by the abandonment of reason and a blind "leap of faith." Like faith, it is a gift from God; and even Jesus Christ, Himself, when He was here as a man on the earth, could not give it to others: that was the sole prerogative of His Father in heaven. All of this is vividly exemplified in the following passage regarding an incident that took place probably after Jesus had already been with His disciples for more than two of the three years He was to have with them. He became increasingly conscious of what lay ahead in Jerusalem, for Him of sufferings and for them of trials, and was concerned as to whether anything fundamental was yet done in them which would suffice to carry them through.

> Now when Jesus came into the parts of Caesarea Philippi, he asked his disciples, saying, Who do men say that the Son of man is? And they said, Some say John the Baptist; some, Elijah; and others, Jeremiah, or one of the prophets. He saith unto them, But who say ye that I am? And Simon Peter answered and said, Thou art the Christ, the Son of the living God. And Jesus answered and said unto him, Blessed art thou, Simon Bar-Jonah: for flesh and blood hath not revealed it unto thee, but my Father who is in heaven. And I also say unto thee, that thou art Peter [πέτρος *petros*, a small rock or stone], and upon this rock [πέτρα *petra*, a rock or massive cliff] I will build my church; and the gates of Hades shall not prevail against it. (Matt 16:13-18)

Was He apprehensive about putting the question directly to His disciples, and so led up to it gently by enquiring first about others? After all, everything in the future hung upon there being something wrought in the disciples that would be adequate to carry them through the trauma of His rejection and crucifixion, and then provide the foundation for the church. But when He puts the question to them directly, it is at once apparent to Him, from Peter's reply, that revelation had been granted by His Father. Peter (*petros*), a little stone, had received the massive, immovable cliff (*petra*) of revelation. It was upon this immovable cliff—spiritual revelation—that Christ would build His church.

Appendix A

This appendix contains two excerpts from the works of Augustine and one from those of Thomas Aquinas.

The first by Augustine is a reasoned piece in which he seeks to refute the Pelagian accusation that he and others like him, when they speak of grace, are really indicating fate. It is instructive that, despite all the reasoning and when all is said and done, the issue is still far from clear. What does seem clear, however, is that infant baptism* is a questionable practice. How can one reconcile the idea of a child of godly parents who dies at childbirth before being baptized thereby suffering spiritual loss, and the child of ungodly parents who by chance is baptized before death thereby receiving blessing, with the notion of a God of love who is just? Reasoning in this manner raises more questions than it answers. It is interesting to study the Gospels with this in mind: the Scribes, Pharisees, and Sadducees put questions to Jesus that were designed to provoke him into an argument with them. He only ever had to answer once, however—it was always a spiritual answer that went to the root of the motive in the questioner's heart. These persons never pursued matters further with Him.

The second excerpt from Augustine's works is his exposition of verses from First John. Here Augustine writes out of spiritual experience, and the tone is quite different—there is no dispute or argument, he is simply pronouncing what he knows to be true.

The third excerpt, from the works of Thomas Aquinas, is a homily on the famous verse, so often quoted, from John: "For God so loved the world, that he gave his only begotten Son, that whosoever believeth on him should not perish, but have eternal life." (Jn 3:16) This verse is at the very heart

---

*The idea of baptismal regeneration is not originally Christian but is found in a number of ancient pagan religions. See Hislop, *The Two Babylons* (London: S. W. Partridge & Co., 1916) 129-44.

of the Gospel. Aquinas's treatment of it, while true, is rather academic and reasoned, however; and even though it is called a homily it has little homiletic appeal.

Chapter 10
WHY THE PELAGIANS FALSELY ACCUSE CATHOLICS
OF MAINTAINING FATE UNDER THE NAME OF GRACE

But, as I was somewhat more attentively considering for what reason they should think it well to object this to us, that we assert fate under the name of grace, I first of all looked into those words of theirs which follow. For thus they have thought that this was to be objected to us: "Under the name," say they, "of grace, they so assert fate as to say that unless God inspired unwilling and resisting man with the desire of good, and that good imperfect, he would neither be able to decline from evil nor to lay hold of good." Then a little after, where they mention what they maintain, I gave heed to what was said by them about this matter. "We confess," say they, "that baptism is necessary for all ages, and that grace, moreover, assists the good purpose of everybody; but yet that it does not infuse the love of virtue into a reluctant one, because there is no acceptance of persons with God." [Rom 2:11, Col 3:25] From these words of theirs, I perceived that for this reason they either think, or wish it to be thought, that we assert fate under the name of grace, because we say that God's grace is not given in respect of our merits, but according to His own most merciful will, in that He said, "I will be gracious to whom I will be gracious, and will show mercy on whom I will show mercy." [Exod 33:19, Rom 9:15] Where, by way of consequence, it is added, "Therefore it is not of him that willeth, nor of him that runneth, but of God that showeth mercy." [Rom 9:16] Here any one might be equally foolish in thinking or saying that the apostle is an assertor of fate. But here these people sufficiently lay themselves open; for when they malign us by saying that we maintain fate under the name of grace, because we say that God's grace is not given on account of our merits, beyond a doubt they confess that they themselves say that it is given on account of our merits; thus their blindness could not conceal and dissimulate that they believe and think thus, although, when this view was objected to him, Pelagius, in the episcopal judgment of Palestine, with crafty fear condemned it. For it was objected to him from the words of his own disciple Cœlestius, indeed, that he himself also was in the habit of saying that God's grace is given on account of our merits. And he in abhorrence, or in pretended abhorrence, of this, did not delay, with his lips at least, to anathematize it; but, as his later writings indicate, and the assertion of those followers of his makes evident, he kept it in his deceitful heart, until afterwards his boldness might put forth in letters what the cunning of a denier had then hidden for fear. And still the Pelagian bishops do not dread, and at least are not ashamed, to send their letters to the catholic Eastern bishops, in which they charge us with being assertors of fate because we do not say that even grace is given according to our merits; although Pelagius, fearing the Eastern bishops, did not dare to say this, and so was compelled to condemn it.

Chapter 11 (6)

THE ACCUSATION OF FATE
IS THROWN BACK UPON THE ADVERSARIES

But is it true, O children of pride, enemies of God's grace, new Pelagian heretics, that whoever says that all man's good deservings are preceded by God's grace, and that God's grace is not given to merits, lest it should not be grace if it is not given freely but be repaid as due to those who deserve it, seems to you to assert fate? Do not you yourselves also say, whatever be your purpose, that baptism is necessary for all ages? Have you not written in this very letter of yours that opinion concerning baptism, and that concerning grace side by side? Why did not baptism, which is given to infants, by that very juxtaposition admonish you what you ought to think concerning grace? For these are your words: "We confess that baptism is necessary for all ages, and that grace, moreover, assists the good purpose of everybody; but yet that it does not infuse the love of virtue into a reluctant one, because there is no acceptance of persons with God." In all these words of yours, I for the meanwhile say nothing of what you have said concerning grace. But give a reason concerning baptism, why you should say that it is necessary for all ages; say why it is necessary for infants. Assuredly because it confers some good upon them; and that same something is neither small nor moderate, but of great account. For although you deny that they contract the original sin which is remitted in baptism, yet you do not deny that in that laver of regeneration they are adopted from the sons of men unto the sons of God; nay, you even preach this. Tell us, then, how the infants, whoever they are, that are baptized in Christ and have departed from the body, received so lofty a gift as this, and with what preceding merits. If you should say that they have deserved this by the piety of their parents, it will be replied to you, Why is this benefit sometimes denied to the children of pious people and given to the children of the wicked? For sometimes the offspring born from religious people, in tender age, and thus fresh from the womb, is fore-stalled by death before it can be washed in the laver of regeneration, and the infant born of Christ's foes is baptized in Christ by the mercy of Christians,—the bap-tized mother bewails her own little one not baptized, and the chaste virgin gathers in to be baptized a foreign offspring, exposed by an unchaste mother. Here, cer-tainly, the merits of parents are wanting, and even by your own confession the merits of the infants themselves are wanting also. For we know that you do not believe this of the human soul, that it has lived somewhere before it inhabited this earthly body, and has done something either of good or of evil for which it might deserve such difference in the flesh. What cause, then, has procured baptism for this infant, and has denied it to that? Do they have fate because they do not have merit? or is there in these things acceptance of persons with God? For you have said both,—first fate, afterwards acceptance of persons,—that, since both must be refuted, there may remain the merit which you wish to introduce against grace. Answer, then, concerning the merits of infants, why some should depart from their bodies baptized, other not baptized, and by the merits of their parents neither pos-sess nor fail of so excellent a gift that they should become sons of God from sons of men, by no deserving of their parents, by no deservings of their own. You are silent, forsooth, and you find yourselves rather in the same position which you object to us. For if when there is no merit you say that consequently there is fate, and on this account wish the merit of man to be understood in the grace of God, lest you should be compelled to confess fate; see, you rather assert a fate in the baptism of infants, since you avow that in them there is no merit. But if, in the case of infants to be baptized, you deny that any merit at all precedes, and yet do not concede that there is a fate, why do you cry out,—when we say that the grace of God is therefore given freely, lest it should not be grace, and is not repaid as if it were due to preceding merits,—that we are assertors of fate?—not perceiving that in the justification of the wicked, as there are no merits because it is God's grace, so that it is not fate because it is God's grace, and so that it is not acceptance of persons because it is God's grace.

Chapter 12
WHAT IS MEANT UNDER THE NAME OF FATE

Because they who affirm fate contend that not only actions and events, but, more-over, our very wills themselves depend on the position of the stars at the time in which one is conceived or born; which positions they call "constellations." But the grace of God stands above not only all stars and all heavens, but, moreover, all angels. In a word, the assertors of fate attribute both men's good and evil doings and fortunes to fate; but God in the ill fortunes of men follows up their merits with due retribution, while good fortunes He bestows by undeserved grace with a merciful will; doing both the one and the other not according to a temporal conjunction of stars, but according to eternal and high counsel of His severity and goodness. We see, then, that neither belongs to fate. Here, if you answer that this very benevolence of God, by which He follows not merits, but bestows undeserved benefits with gratuitous bounty, should rather be called "fate," when the apostle calls this "grace," saying, "By grace are ye saved through faith; and that not of yourselves, but it is the gift of God; not of works, lest perchance any one should be lifted up,"--do you not consider, do you not perceive, that it is not by us that fate is asserted under the name of grace, but it is rather by you that divine grace is called by the name of fate?*

SECOND EXCERPT FROM AUGUSTINE

From
HOMILY 3—1 JOHN 2:18-27

13. "And ye have not need that any man teach you, because His unction teacheth you concerning all things." Then to what purpose is it that "we," my brethren, teach you? If "His unction teacheth you concerning all things," it seems we labor without a cause. And what mean we, to cry out as we do? Let us leave you to His unction and let His unction teach you. But this is putting the question only to myself: I put it also to that same apostle: let him deign to hear a babe that asks of him: to John himself I say, Had those the unction to whom thou wast speaking? Thou hast said, "His unction teacheth you concerning all things." To what purpose hast thou written an Epistle like this? what teaching didst "thou" give them? what instruction? what edification? See here now, brethren, see a mighty mystery. The sound of our words strikes the ears, the Master is within. Do not suppose that any man learns ought from man. We can admonish by the sound of our voice; if there be not One within that shall teach, vain is the noise we make. Aye, brethren, have ye a mind to know it? Have ye not all heard this present discourse? and yet how

---

*Augustine, from "Contra duas epistolas pelagianorum" ("Against Two Letters of the Pelagians"), bk. 2, chaps. 10-12, in *A Select Library of the Nicene and Post-Nicene Fathers of the Christian Church,* American edition ed. Philip Schaff, 1st ser. vol. 5 (New York: Christian Literature Company, 1887; repr. Grand Rapids MI: Eerdmans, 1971, 1980) 395-96.

many will go from this place untaught! I, for my part, have spoken to all; but they to whom that Unction within speaketh not, they whom the Holy Ghost within teacheth not, those go back untaught. The teachings of the master from without are a sort of aids and admonitions. He that teacheth the hearts, hath His chair in heaven. Therefore saith He also Himself in the Gospel: "Call no man your master upon earth; One is your Master, even Christ." Let Him therefore Himself speak to you within, when not one of mankind is there: for though there be some one at thy side, there is none in thine heart. Yet let there not be none in thine heart: let Christ be in thine heart: let His unction be in the heart, lest it be a heart thirsting in the wilderness, and having no fountains to be watered withal. There is then, I say, a Master within that teacheth: Christ teacheth; His inspiration teacheth. Where His inspiration and His unction is not, in vain do words make a noise from without. So are the words, brethren, which we speak from without, as is the husband-man to the tree: from without he worketh, applieth water and diligence of culture; let him from without apply what he will, does he form the apples? does he do any thing like this from within? But whose doing is this? Hear the husbandman, the apostle: both see what we are, and hear the Master within: "I have planted, Apollos hath watered; but God gave the increase: neither he that planteth is any thing, neither he that watereth, but He that giveth the increase, even God." This then we say to you: whether we plant, or whether we water, by speaking we are not any thing; but He that giveth the increase, even God: that is, "His unction which teacheth you concerning all things."

From
HOMILY 4—1 JOHN 2:27; 3:8

1. Ye remember, brethren, that yesterday's lesson was brought to a close at this point, that "ye have no need that any man teach you, but the unction itself teacheth you concerning all things." Now this, as I am sure ye remember, we so expounded to you, that we who from without speak to your ears, are as workmen applying culture from without to a tree, but we cannot give the increase nor form the fruits: but only He that created and redeemed and called you, He, dwelling in you by faith and the Spirit, must speak to you within, else vain is all our noise of words. Whence does this appear? From this: that while many hear, not all are persuaded of that which is said, but only they to whom God speaks within. Now they to whom He speaks within, are those who give place to Him: and those give place to God, who "give not place to the devil." For the devil wishes to inhabit the hearts of men, and speak there the things which are able to seduce. But what saith

the Lord Jesus? "The prince of this world is cast out." Whence cast? out of heaven and earth? out of the fabric of the world? Nay, but out of the hearts of the believing. The invader being cast out, let the Redeemer dwell within: because the same redeemed, who created. And the devil now assaults from without, not conquers Him that hath possession within. And he assaults from without, by casting in various temptations: but that person consents not thereto, to whom God speaks within, and the unction of which ye have heard.

2. "And it is true," namely, this same unction; i.e., the very Spirit of the Lord which teacheth men, cannot lie: "and is not false. Even as it hath taught you, abide ye in the same. And now, little children, abide ye in Him, that when He shall be manifested, we may have boldness in His sight, that we be not put to shame by Him at His coming." Ye see, brethren: we believe on Jesus whom we have not seen: they announced Him, that saw, that handled, that heard the word out of His own mouth and that they might persuade all mankind of the truth thereof, they were sent by Him, not dared to go of themselves. And whither were they sent? Ye heard while the Gospel was read, "Go, preach the Gospel to the whole creation which is under heaven." Consequently, the disciples were sent "every where:" with signs and wonders to attest that what they spake, they had seen. And we believe on Him whom we have not seen, and we look for Him to come. Whoso look for Him by faith, shall rejoice when He cometh: those who are without faith, when that which now they see not is come, shall be ashamed. And that confusion of face shall not be for a single day and so pass away, in such sort as those are wont to be confounded, who are found out in some fault, and are scoffed at by their fellow-men. That confusion shall carry them that are confounded to the left hand, that to them it may be said, "Go into everlasting fire, prepared for the devil and his angels." Let us abide then in His words, that we be not confounded when He cometh. For Himself saith in the Gospel to them that had believed on Him: "If ye shall abide in my word, then are ye verily my disciples." And, as if they had asked, With what fruit? "And," saith He, "ye shall know the truth, and the truth shall make you free." For as yet our salvation is in hope, not in deed: for we do not already possess that which is promised, but we hope for it to come. And "faithful is He that promised"; He deceiveth not thee: only do thou not faint, but wait for the promise. For He, the Truth, cannot deceive. Be not thou a liar, to profess one thing and do another; keep thou the faith, and He keeps His promise. But if thou keep not the faith, thine own self, not He that promised, hath defrauded thee.*

---

*Augustine, from "Ten Homilies on the Epistle of John to the Parthians," in *A Select*

AQUINAS

THE GREATEST OF DIVINE LOVE

"God so loved the world, as to give His only begotten Son; that whosoever believeth in Him, may have everlasting life." (John 3:16)

The cause of all good things is the Lord and Divine love. For to wish good to anyone belongs to love. Since therefore, the will of God is the cause of things, from this very fact, good comes to us because God loves us. The love of God is also the cause of the good in nature. Likewise, it is the cause of the good resulting from grace. 'I have loved you with an everlasting love, therefore, I have drawn thee,'' namely through the grace of God.

That God is the Giver of the good resulting from grace also proceeds from His immense charity and hence, it will be shown here, that this charity of God is the greatest charity and this because of four reasons:

1. Because of the Person loving, for it is God Who loves and loves exceedingly. Therefore He says, "God so loved."

2. God's love is the greatest because of the condition of the person loved, for it is man who is the object of God's love, the worldly man living in sin. "God commendeth His charity towards us, because when as yet we were His enemies, we were reconciled to God, by the death of His Son." (Rom. 5:10) Hence it is written, "God so loved the world."

3. God's love is the greatest because of the greatness of His gifts, for love is shown by a gift, as Gregory says, "The proof of love is in the manifestation of action." But God gave us the greatest gift for He gave us His only begotten Son, His own Son, Son by nature, consubstantial, not adopted, but only begotten Son. God gave Him to us to prove the immensity of His love.

4. God's love is the greatest because of the magnitude of its effects, because through it we receive eternal life. Wherefor it is written, "Whosoever believeth in Him may not perish, but have life everlasting"; which He has obtained for us through His death on the Cross.

Something is said to perish when it is prevented from obtaining the end for which it was created. But man is created and ordained for eternal life and as long as he

Library of the Nicene and Post-Nicene Fathers of the Christian Church, ed. Philip Schaff, 1st ser. vol. 7 (1887; repr. New York: Charles Scribner's Sons, 1908; repr. Grand Rapids MI: Eerdmans, 1971, 1980, 1983) 481-82.

sins he is turned away from that destined end. Still, while he lives, he does not perish entirely for he can yet be saved through God's grace and mercy; but if he dies in sin then he perishes completely.

The immensity of Divine Love is referred to by our Lord when he says "that whosoever believeth in Him, may not perish, but may have life everlasting." For God in giving eternal life gave Himself to us, because eternal life is nothing other than to enjoy God forever. Moreover, to give oneself to God is a sign of great love. (In John 3)*

---

*Thomas Aquinas, *Meditations,* adapted by E. C. Mceniry, O.P. (Columbus OH: College Book Company, 1941) 3-4.

Appendix B

Works of Pascal

THE MYSTERY OF JESUS*

Jesus suffers in His passion the torments which men inflict upon Him; but in His agony he suffers the torments which He brings upon Himself: *turbare semetipsum* [to thrust oneself into distress]. It is a suffering inflicted not by a human, but by an all-powerful hand, and only One who is all-powerful could bear it.

Jesus seeks at least some comfort from His three dearest friends, and they sleep. He begs them to support Him a little, and they leave Him with complete indifference, not having enough compassion to prevent them sleeping, even for a moment. And thus Jesus was abandoned, all alone, to the wrath of God.

Jesus is alone on the earth; not only is there no one who feels and shares His suffering, but no one knows it: heaven and He alone share this knowledge.

Jesus is in a garden, not of delights as the first Adam, where he lost himself and the whole human race, but in a garden of torment, where He saved Himself and the whole human race.

---

*Blaise Pascal, "Le mystère de Jésus," in *Oeuvres complètes. Texte établi et annoté par Jacques Chevalier,* Bibliothèque de la Pléiade 34 (Paris: Éditions Gallimard, 1954) 1312-15. As an alternative translation, cf. "The Mystery of Jesus" (from "Fragments in the *Recueil original*"), in *Pascal Pensées,* trans. A. J. Krailsheimer, Penguin Classics (Baltimore MD: Penguin Books, 1966) 312-20; Krailsheimer's translation follows the order of the several editions of Pascal by M. Louis Lafuma (1952, 1962, 1963)—which order differs from the Chevalier edition followed here—and thus includes additional "fragments" of text.

He suffers this affliction and this forsakenness in the horror of night.

I believe that Jesus never complained except on this one occasion; but then He complained as if He could no longer bear His excessive suffering: "My soul is sorrowful, even unto death."

Jesus seeks companionship and comfort from men. It seems to me that this is the only occasion during His whole life. But He receives none, for His disciples are asleep.

Jesus will be in agony even until the end of the world: We must not sleep during that time.

In the midst of this universal abandonment, which includes that of His friends whom He chose to watch with Him, finding them sleeping He is distressed because of the peril to which they expose, not Him, but themselves. He admonishes them for their own safety and good, with sincere love for them even whilst they are ungrateful, and warns them that the spirit is willing and the flesh is weak.

Finding them still asleep, unrestrained from sleep by any consideration for Him or for themselves, Jesus has the kindness not to waken them, and leaves them to rest.

Jesus prays, uncertain of the will of the Father, and is afraid of death; but, as soon as He knows it [the will of the Father], He goes forward to offer Himself to death. *Eamus. Processit* [Let us follow. He had gone ahead.] (John).

Jesus asked of men, and was not heard.

While His disciples slept, Jesus wrought their Salvation. He has wrought the same for every one of the righteous while they slept, both in their nothingness before their birth, and in their sins after it.

He prays only once that the cup may pass from Him; and twice that it come if necessary.

Jesus is weary.

Seeing all his friends asleep and all his enemies watchful, Jesus commits Himself entirely to His Father.

Jesus does not look at the enmity in Judas, but at the order of God, which He loves—He is so little affected by the enmity that He calls him friend.

Jesus tears Himself away from His disciples in order to enter into His agony; we must tear ourselves away from our nearest and dearest so as to imitate Him.

Jesus being in agony and in the greatest affliction, let us pray longer.

We beg mercy of God, not that He may leave us at peace in our vices, but that He may deliver us from them.

If God gave us masters by His hand, oh! how gladly should we obey them! Constraint and events follow unfailingly.

—"Comfort yourself, you would not seek Me if you had not found Me.

"I thought of you in My agony, I sweated such drops of blood for you.

"It is tempting Me rather than proving yourself when you ponder if you will do such and such a thing on a given occasion; I shall act in you if the occasion arises.

"Let yourself be guided by my rules; see how well I have led the Virgin and the saints who let me act in them.

"The Father loves all that I do.

"Do you wish that it always cost me some of the blood of My humanity, without your shedding tears.

"Your conversion is my business; fear not, and pray with confidence as for Me.

"I am present with you through My word in the Scripture, through my spirit in the Church and through inspirations, through My power in the priests, through My prayer in the faithful.

"Physicians will not heal you; for in the end you will die. But it is I who heal, and make the body immortal.

"Suffer chains and bodily slavery; at present I only deliver you from spiritual bondage.

"I am more a friend to you than are any others; for I have done more for you than have they, and they would not suffer what I have suffered for you, nor would they have died for you at the time when you were unfaithful and remorseless as did I, and as I am ready to do, and do, in My elect and at the Holy Sacrament.

"If you knew your sins, you would lose heart.

—I shall lose it then Lord, for, as You assure me of the fact, I believe their maliciousness.

"No, for I, from whom you learn this, can cure you of them, and my very telling you is a sign that I wish to cure you. In the measure that you expiate them, you will know them, and it will be said to you: Behold the sins which are forgiven you. Repent therefore for your hidden sins and for the hidden maliciousness of the sins you know.

—Lord I give you all.

"I love you more fervently than you have loved your defilements, *ut immundus pro luto* [how man, who is unclean, loves the dirt].

"Let the glory be Mine and not yours, worm and earth.

"Testify to your director that My own words are an occasion of evil to you, or of vanity or curiosity.

—I see the depths of my pride, curiosity and concupiscence. There is no righteous relationship either between me and God or between me and Jesus Christ. But He was made sin by me, all your plagues fell upon Him. He is more abominable than I, and, far from abhorring me, He counts Himself honored that I go to Him and help Him. But He healed Himself, which is all the more reason why He will heal me. I must add my wounds to His, and unite myself to Him, and He will save me by saving Himself. But I must not add any [wounds] in the future.

Eritis sicut dii scientes bonum et malum [Ye shall be as gods, knowing good and evil]. Everyone plays God in judging: "That is good or bad," and in grieving or rejoicing too much from events.

Do little things as though they were big, on account of the majesty of Jesus Christ who does them in us, and who lives our life; and do the big things as if they were little and easy because of His omnipotence.

"Don't compare yourself to others but to Me. If you don't find Me in those to whom you are comparing yourself, you are comparing yourself to one who is loathsome. If you find Me in them, compare yourself to Me. But what comparison will you make? Will it be you or Me in You? If it is you, it is a loathsome person. If it is I, you compare Me to Myself. Now, I am God in everything.

"I speak to you and counsel you often, because your guide [director] cannot speak to you, for I do not want you to be without a guide. And perhaps I do it in answer to his prayers, and thus he [the guide] leads you without your seeing it.

"You would not seek Me if you did not possess Me. Therefore, be not troubled."

CONCERNING THE CONVERSION OF THE SINNER*

The first thing that God breathes into the soul, which he condescends to touch with reality, is a knowledge and a quite unusual insight, as a consequence of which the soul looks upon things and itself in an altogether different manner.

This new light makes the soul fearful, and creates an uneasiness which disturbs the peace it used to experience in those things that formerly caused its delight.

It can no longer peacefully enjoy the things which once charmed it. Unrelenting scruples disturb it in this enjoyment, and this inner perception deprives the soul of the charms to which it was accustomed to abandon itself with an uninhibited heart.

But the soul finds even more grief in the practice of piety than in the world's vanities. On the one hand, the presence of visible objects affects it more than the hope of invisible ones, and, on the other, the stability of the invisible ones touches it more than the vanity of the visible. Thus the presence of the ones and the stability of the others vie for its affection; and the vanity of the ones and the absence of the others arouse its aversion; with the result that there is created in the soul a disorder and confusion which [it has difficulty in resolving, but which is the consequence of former impressions longtime felt, and of new ones which it is experiencing.]

The soul now regards perishable things as perishing, and even already perished; and, in the light of the certain destruction of everything it loves, it becomes fearful, seeing that each moment deprives it further of the enjoyment of its possessions, and that what is most dear to it is slipping away all the time, and that finally a day will surely come when it will find itself totally stripped of all the things on which it had set its hopes. Consequently it understands perfectly that, as its heart

---

*Blaise Pascal, "Sur la conversion du pécheur," in the section entitled "Opuscules" ("Minor Works") in *Oeuvres complètes,* 548-52. The original text had several "unfinished" paragraphs, and several gaps where words had been erased by Pascal. (See my explanation, above, pp. 92-93, why Pascal probably did not write this work. For its first 100 years it was attributed, rightly I believe, to his sister Jacqueline.) Text enclosed in brackets in this translation represents the additions, corrections, or reinsertions of a copyist and/or editor. As an alternative translation (lacking later editorial additions and thus with several large "gaps"), cf. "On the Conversion of the Sinner," trans. O. W. Wight, in *Blaise Pascal: Thoughts, Letters, Minor Works,* trans. W. F. Trotter, M. L. Booth, and O. W. Wight, Harvard Classics 48 (New York: P. F. Collier & Son, 1910) 388-91; Wight's translation is based on the 1904-1914 edition of the original text edited by Léon Brunschvicg, P. Boutroux, and F. Gazier.

is only attached to fragile and vain things, its soul is bound to find itself alone and abandoned on leaving this life, since it has not taken the precaution of uniting itself to some good that is genuine and subsists by itself, which could have sustained it both during and after this life.

As a consequence the soul begins to reckon as nothing everything that must return to nothingness, heaven, earth, its mind, body, relatives, friends, enemies, and goods, poverty, affliction, prosperity, honor, shame, esteem, scorn, authority, indigence, health, sickness, and life itself: in short, everything that must last a shorter time than its soul is incapable of fulfilling the purposes of this soul which seeks earnestly to become established in a happiness as lasting as itself.

The soul begins to be amazed at the blindness in which it formerly lived; and when it considers, on the one hand, the long period it lived without reflecting on these matters, and the great number of persons who live in this way, and on the other, how it is an established fact that the soul, immortal as it is, cannot find its happiness amid perishable things which will be taken from it at the latest at death, it enters into holy confusion and into a disturbed state which evokes a very salutory unrest.

For it recognizes that however great may be the number of those who grow old in the maxims of the world, and whatever authority this multitude of examples of those who place their happiness in the world may have, it is nontheless certain that, even if the things of the world offered some substantial pleasure (which is proven to be not the case by an infinite number of such distressing and continuous experiences) we shall inevitably lose these things, or be deprived of them at death. Consequently, as the soul has amassed to itself treasures of temporal goods (of whatever sort they may be—gold, knowledge, or reputation) it is absolutely necessary that it be stripped of all these objects of its happiness, because, if they did bring a measure of satisfaction to the soul, they will not be able to satisfy it for ever; and even if they produce real happiness, that happiness is not lasting since it must be limited to the duration of this life.

And so, by a holy humility, which God exalts above arrogance, the soul begins to rise above the general run of men. It condemns their conduct, detests their maxims, laments their blindness. It devotes itself to the quest for the real good: It understands that this good must have two qualities—one, that it last as long as the soul itself, and that it cannot be taken from the soul except by its consent; and the other, that there be nothing more pleasing.

The soul observes that when, in its blindness, it loved the world, it found this second quality in it, because it knew nothing more pleasing; but, as the soul does not find the first quality in the world, it knows it is not the highest good. The soul therefore seeks this latter elsewhere, and knows by a perfectly pure light that this good is not in the things which are in the soul, nor outside it, nor before it (nothing therefore in it or around it), the soul begins to seek it above.

This upward movement is so lofty and transcendent that it does not stop at the sky (there is nothing there to satisfy the soul), nor above the sky, nor amongst the angels, nor amongst the most perfect beings. The soul passes beyond all created beings, and cannot satisfy its heart until it has reached the throne of God where it begins to find its rest and this good which is incomparable in its pleasingness, and which cannot be taken away from it except by its own consent.

For although the soul does not experience those charms with which God recompenses habitual piety, it nevertheless understands that created beings cannot be more pleasing than the Creator; and its reason, guided by the illumination of grace, makes it understand that there is nothing more pleasing than God, and that He can only be taken away from those who reject Him, since to desire Him is to possess Him, and to refuse Him is to lose Him.

Thus the soul rejoices at having found a good which cannot be taken from it as long as the soul desires it—a good which has nothing above it. And, amid these new thoughts, the soul comes in view of the greatness of its Creator, and enters into deep humiliations and worship. Consequently the soul humbles itself, and, unable to form a low enough opinion of itself, or to conceive a lofty enough one of this highest good, it renews its efforts to humble itself to the bottommost depths of nothingness, while thinking on the boundlessness of God which it multiplies ceaselessly. Finally, in view of all this, which exhausts its strength, the soul worships Him in silence, considers itself His vile and useless creature, and by repeated reverences worships and blesses Him; and would wish to bless Him and worship Him for ever.

After this, the soul recognizes the grace He has bestowed upon it in manifesting His infinite majesty to such a wretched worm; and, after making a firm resolution to be eternally grateful for this, it becomes ashamed at having preferred so many vanities to this divine master, and, in a spirit of remorse and penitence, it appeals to His compassion in order to arrest His anger, the effect of which seems fearsome in the light of His vastness. . . .

The soul prays ardently to God to obtain by His mercy, that, as it pleased Him to reveal Himself to the soul, it may please Him to lead it and to grant it an understanding of the means by which it may reach Him. For, as it is towards God that the soul aspires, it aspires furthermore to reach Him using only those means which come from God Himself, because it wishes that He, Himself, may be its path, its aim, and its ultimate end. Following these prayers, the soul [understands that it must act in conformity with its new light].

The soul begins to know God, and desires to reach Him, but, being ignorant of the means of accomplishing this it does the same thing, if its desire is sincere and true, as would a person who, desirous of reaching a certain place, but having lost his way and being aware of the fact, would seek the help of those who knew the way perfectly. [The soul likewise consults with those who can instruct it in the way which leads to God, which way it for so long a time abandoned. But in asking to know it,] the soul resolves to conform to His will for the rest of its life; but, as its natural weakness, together with the habit of sinning in which it has lived, have made it powerless to attain this happiness, it implores of His mercy the means of reaching Him, of attaching itself to Him, and of cleaving to Him eternally. [Totally absorbed with this beauty which is both so old and so new to it, the soul feels that all its movements must be directed towards this end.]

Thus the soul recognizes that it must worship God, as should a creature, render thanks to Him as one that is indebted, make amends to Him as someone guilty, and pray to Him as one who is needy[, until it can no longer do other than see Him, love Him and praise Him for ever].

Index